CENTRE FOR EDUCATIONAL RESEARCH AND INNOVATION

Schooling for Tomorrow

# Think Scenarios, Rethink Education

OECD

ORGANISATION FOR ECONOMIC CO-OPERATION AND DEVELOPMENT

# ORGANISATION FOR ECONOMIC CO-OPERATION AND DEVELOPMENT

The OECD is a unique forum where the governments of 30 democracies work together to address the economic, social and environmental challenges of globalisation. The OECD is also at the forefront of efforts to understand and to help governments respond to new developments and concerns, such as corporate governance, the information economy and the challenges of an ageing population. The Organisation provides a setting where governments can compare policy experiences, seek answers to common problems, identify good practice and work to co-ordinate domestic and international policies.

The OECD member countries are: Australia, Austria, Belgium, Canada, the Czech Republic, Denmark, Finland, France, Germany, Greece, Hungary, Iceland, Ireland, Italy, Japan, Korea, Luxembourg, Mexico, the Netherlands, New Zealand, Norway, Poland, Portugal, the Slovak Republic, Spain, Sweden, Switzerland, Turkey, the United Kingdom and the United States. The Commission of the European Communities takes part in the work of the OECD.

OECD Publishing disseminates widely the results of the Organisation's statistics gathering and research on economic, social and environmental issues, as well as the conventions, guidelines and standards agreed by its members.

---

*This work is published on the responsibility of the Secretary-General of the OECD. The opinions expressed and arguments employed herein do not necessarily reflect the official views of the Organisation or of the governments of its member countries.*

---

*Also available in French under the title:*
**Repenser l'enseignement : Des scénarios pour agir**

© OECD 2006

No reproduction, copy, transmission or translation of this publication may be made without written permission. Applications should be sent to OECD Publishing: *rights@oecd.org* or by fax (33 1) 45 24 13 91. Permission to photocopy a portion of this work should be addressed to the Centre français d'exploitation du droit de copie, 20, rue des Grands-Augustins, 75006 Paris, France (*contact@cfcopies.com*).

# Foreword

Today's world is increasingly complex and uncertain, with a growing number of stakeholders making new demands on education. Yet, so much of education is still determined by short-term thinking – preoccupation with pressing immediate problems or simply seeking more efficient ways of maintaining established practice. Neglect of the long term is increasingly problematic in meeting the challenges of complexity and change.

People working in education at all levels thus need to be able to look beyond the straitjackets of immediate constraints. Scenarios can stimulate reflection on the major changes taking place in education and its wider environment. They help to clarify our visions of what we would like schooling to be and how to get there, and the undesirable futures we wish to avoid. Futures thinking in general provides tools to engage in strategic dialogue, even among those who might usually be worlds apart. It is about helping us to shape, not predict, the future.

There are various definitions of "scenario" to choose from and a good one is proposed by Philip van Notten in Chapter 4: *"Scenarios are consistent and coherent descriptions of alternative hypothetical futures that reflect different perspectives on past, present, and future developments, which can serve as a basis for action."* But as his and the other chapters make clear, the scenarios themselves are only one element in the larger futures processes aimed at opening new horizons, clarifying visions, and informing strategic thinking. These tools and processes together are the subject of this report.

This volume has been produced by the "Schooling for Tomorrow" programme in OECD's Centre for Educational Research and Innovation (CERI).[1] Since its launch at an international conference in Hiroshima in the 1990s, "Schooling for Tomorrow" has completed two phases and is now embarked on its third, still more ambitious phase. This report is the main output on futures thinking from the completed Phase Two. This phase centred around a small number of volunteer "inner-core" systems exploring how

---

[1] Other titles in the *Schooling for Tomorrow* Series are: *Personalising Education* (2006); *Networks of Innovation: Towards New Models for Managing Schools and Systems* (2003); *What Schools for the Future?* (2001); *Learning to Change: ICT in Schools* (2001); *Learning to Bridge the Digital Divide* (2000); *Innovating Schools* (1999).

scenario methods can inform concrete challenges for educational leadership and policy-making. It also reviewed alternative approaches. The two main international events during this phase were the "Schooling for Tomorrow" Forums held near Poitiers, France in February 2003 and in Toronto in June 2004. Some of the chapters have been developed out of presentations made in Toronto, to which others have subsequently been added.

Phase One laid the ground with the creation of schooling scenarios, which set has been a central reference point ever since:

*Attempting to maintain the status quo*
1. The "Bureaucratic School Systems Continue" Scenario

*Diverse, dynamic schools after root-and-branch reform* ("re-schooling")
2. The "Schools as Focused Learning Organisations" Scenario
3. The "Schools as Core Social Centres" Scenario

*Systems pursue alternatives to school or disband…* ("de-schooling")
4. The "Extending the Market Model" Scenario
5. The "Learning Networks and the Network Society" Scenario

*…or disintegrate in crisis*
6. The "Teacher Exodus and System Meltdown" Scenario.

These scenarios, together with an analysis of trends and a collection of expert papers, are contained in "*What Schools for the Future?*" (2001). In addition to the scenarios, Phase One included analyses of innovation, networks and the role of technology in education.

We have now entered the third phase. We have significantly broadened active participation with new countries joining the project, committed to much more systematic reporting and evaluation than hitherto. We are putting together new materials as resources for those in different countries undertaking futures work in education. Through all these elements, an international knowledge base of educational futures thinking is being constructed at the core of Phase Three.

Within the OECD, the "Schooling for Tomorrow" project leader, Senior Analyst David Istance, was responsible for putting this report together, along with Henno Theisens. Riel Miller, formerly of CERI, made an important contribution to Phase Two and this report. Delphine Grandrieux and Jennifer Cannon prepared and edited the text for publication and an earlier editorial contribution was made by consultant Edna Ruth Yahil. This report is published under the responsibility of the Secretary-General of OECD.

Anne-Barbara Ischinger
Director for Education

# ACKNOWLEDGEMENTS

We would like to acknowledge the lead taken by the volunteer systems who implemented "futures thinking in action" initiatives as described in Part Two below. Many people have been involved in these initiatives who cannot be mentioned individually. So, our collective thanks extend to the teams and participants from:

England's FutureSight project, particularly, the National College for School Leadership (NCSL), the Innovation Unit at the Department for Education and Skills (DfES), and the think-tank Demos;

The Netherlands study team from the Ministry of Education, Culture and Science; the Dutch Principals Academy; and the KPC Group;

The New Zealand "Secondary Futures" programme; and

The Ontario Ministry of Education, Canada, and the "Teaching as a Profession" and "Vision 2020" teams.

We wish we had had this report to share with these teams when they set out on their scenario initiatives. Instead, their explorations and ours at OECD will serve futures initiatives to come as they use these methods to shape their agendas for educational change.

Ontario was the generous host to the 2nd "Schooling for Tomorrow" Toronto Forum which was such an important milestone during Phase Two. Again, too many were involved to mention them all individually but we would like to acknowledge the roles played by Aryeh Gitterman and Denis Vaillancourt, Cheryl Carlson and Marie-France Lefort, and Anna Brunemeyer, Louis Lizotte and Elaine Molgat. Special thanks go to international consultant Tony Mackay for chairing the Toronto conference and for his continuing input to the programme.

We here take the occasion to thank those who hosted the 1st "Schooling for Tomorrow" Forum near Poitiers, France in February 2003; it was out of this event that so much of what is covered in this volume later grew. We wish to acknowledge the particular contributions made by Olivier Cazenave, Nathalie Ingremeau, and Béatrice Revol and by the former project members, Keiko Momii and Cassandra Davis. We are grateful for the support for this event given by the *Conseil Général de la Vienne*, the *Région Poitou-Charentes*, and the Futuroscope Park.

Finally, our acknowledgements go to the individual chapter authors: Tom Bentley, Raymond Daigle, Michael Fullan, Walo Hutmacher, Jonas Svava Iversen, Riel Miller, Philip van Notten, Jay Ogilvy, Jean-Michel Saussois, Hanne Shapiro, and Charles Ungerleider, and to those in the country-based teams who were responsible for drafting the Part Two chapters.

# Table of Contents

**Executive summary** ................................................................................................11

## PART ONE
### CREATING AND USING SCENARIOS TO MAKE A DIFFERENCE IN EDUCATION

**Chapter 1. Education in the information age: scenarios, equity and equality**
by Jay Ogilvy ..............................................................................................................21
    Implementing scenario planning .........................................................................21
    A declaration of educational equality ..................................................................26
    From precision farming to precision schooling ...................................................28
    Differences that make a difference .......................................................................33

**Chapter 2. System thinking, system thinkers and sustainability**
by Michael Fullan ......................................................................................................39
    Change challenges ................................................................................................39
    Systems thinking ...................................................................................................40
    Sustainability .........................................................................................................41
    Concluding remark ...............................................................................................49

**Chapter 3. Scenarios, international comparisons, and key variables for educational scenario analysis**
by Jean-Michel Saussois ............................................................................................53
    Canonic scenarios .................................................................................................53
    The methodological challenge of international comparisons ..............................58
    The normative and socio-technical dimensions ...................................................59
    The four quadrants as scenarios ...........................................................................63
    Moving around the quadrants – what makes for change from one scenario to another .....65

**Chapter 4. Scenario development: a typology of approaches**
by Philip van Notten ...................................................................................................... 69

    What is a scenario? ............................................................................................... 69
    A typology of scenario characteristics ................................................................. 71
    Successful scenarios: cultures of curiosity ........................................................... 84
    Some reflections: scenarios for the very long term .............................................. 86
    Conclusion ............................................................................................................. 87

**Chapter 5. Futures studies, scenarios, and the "possibility-space" approach**
by Riel Miller ................................................................................................................. 93

    Thinking rigorously about the future .................................................................... 93
    Trend- and preference-based scenarios ................................................................ 98
    Possibility-space scenarios ................................................................................. 100

**Chapter 6. Futures thinking methodologies and options for education**
by Jonas Svava Iversen ................................................................................................ 107

    Delineation and mapping .................................................................................... 107
    Identification of critical issues and trends .......................................................... 109
    Scenario creation ................................................................................................ 111
    Using the scenarios ............................................................................................. 116
    Conclusions – enhancing success in using scenarios ......................................... 118

### PART TWO
### FUTURES THINKING IN ACTION

**Chapter 7. England: using scenarios to build capacity for leadership** ................ 123

    Systems and policy context ................................................................................ 123
    Goals of initiatives ............................................................................................. 124
    Process design .................................................................................................... 125
    Scenario content ................................................................................................. 126
    Scenario usage ................................................................................................... 128
    Outcomes ............................................................................................................ 129
    Implications for policy makers .......................................................................... 131

**Chapter 8. The Netherlands: futures thinking in innovation, school organisation and leadership development** ....................................................................................... 133

    Introduction ........................................................................................................ 133
    New educational governance .............................................................................. 134
    The development of visionary school leadership .............................................. 136
    Slash/21: a re-engineered school model ............................................................ 139
    Conclusions ........................................................................................................ 144

## Chapter 9. New Zealand: the Secondary Futures project .......... 145

Process design .......... 146
Further developments after the early design .......... 148
Building on the evidence of the Secondary Futures workshops .......... 151
Feedback and reflection .......... 153

## Chapter 10. Ontario (English-speaking system): the future of "Teaching as a Profession" .......... 155

Introduction .......... 155
The reform context .......... 156
The task .......... 157
The Ontario system .......... 158
The goals of the initiatives .......... 159
Process design .......... 160
Scenario content .......... 163
Outcomes and benefits .......... 165

## Chapter 11. Ontario (French-speaking system): the *Vision 2020* initiative .......... 167

Introduction and background .......... 167
The provincial context .......... 168
Goals of the initiative .......... 169
Process and implementation .......... 169
Outcomes and analysis .......... 171
Development of methods for planning and organising consultations .......... 178
Use of the OECD scenarios .......... 179
Conclusion .......... 181

## Chapter 12. Reflections on the practice and potential of futures thinking .......... 183

Futures thinking to clarify value differences (Charles Ungerleider) .......... 184
Do schools need to be reformed or reinvented? (Raymond Daigle) .......... 187
Consolidate the foundations of evidence-based futures thinking (Walo Hutmacher) .. 190
Broadening horizons, approaches and participants in futures thinking (Hanne Shapiro) 192
Using futures thinking strategically: inward and outward-facing
processes (Tom Bentley) .......... 196

# Executive summary

What happens today in education profoundly influences the lives of individuals and the health of whole communities for decades to come. Yet, educational decision-making is mostly about dealing with pressing immediate issues or seeking more efficient ways of maintaining established practice, rather than about shaping the long term. Using scenarios offer one highly promising way to redress this imbalance. To show how, this new volume in the OECD's *Schooling for Tomorrow* series is both theoretical and practical.

## 1. Creating and using scenarios to make a difference in education

Part One identifies key issues and priorities where futures thinking can make a real difference in education, drawing on insights from many fields. It combines authoritative scholarly overviews and practical lessons to be applied.

*Personalised, equitable schools and the scenario approach*

Jay Ogilvy reflects on methods and the different uses of scenarios. In comparing features of education and business, he suggests that educators, faced with strategic choices, prefer talk over action whereas business people tend to opt for immediate action. The discussion elaborates three different uses of scenarios: to provoke strategic conversation; to stimulate genuinely new, visionary thinking; and as a motivator for getting unstuck. He contrasts positive with negative scenarios and proposes that both are needed, albeit with different considerations and uses.

The second part fills in content and illustrates the methodological points. Ogilvy argues that schools bear the scars of their birth in the agricultural and industrial eras. He shows how parallels can be drawn between the challenges facing school decision-making and those of "precision farming". He calls for a much more sustained realisation of equity and equality as essential in the Information Age when access to knowledge is fundamental. And, he argues for applying market principles much more systematically to schooling.

*System thinking and sustaining change
– building capacity*

Leading educational thinker on innovation and change, Michael Fullan, advises that thinking about the future is not enough for decision makers in education; it is also necessary to conceptualise how to change current systems in specific, powerful ways. He adopts the distinction between *technical problems* which the existing knowledge base can cope with and *adaptive challenges* which current knowledge cannot resolve. It is about the latter that he sees the value of the futures work in education. "Systems thinking" is needed but to be practically useful, practitioner-based system *thinkers* must be developed.

The key to moving forward is to enable leaders to become more effective at leading organisations toward greater sustainability who in turn will guide other leaders in the same direction. Fullan defines and then discusses eight elements of sustainability: i) public service with a moral purpose; ii) commitment to changing context at all levels; iii) lateral capacity-building through networks; iv) intelligent accountability and new vertical relationships; v) deep learning; vi) dual commitment to short-term and long-term results; vii) cyclical energising; and viii) the long lever of leadership.

*Value and supply trends leading to
educational scenarios*

Jean-Michel Saussois presents basic features of scenarios as "ideal types" and the steps involved in developing them, looking at both their evolution and applications in the business world and their relevance and value for educational decision-making. He suggests that demanding assumptions are involved, especially when the exercise is one of international comparison. This may be considered as about matching the *map* and the *territory,* where to design a scenario is to act as a "map-maker".

Saussois presents a two-dimensional framework within which to analyse the trends and futures for schooling – the shifting *values* about where schools belong in the social fabric and the *delivery or supply* function of schooling. The values line goes from where education is socially oriented to where it is individualistically oriented as schooling is geared to its "clients" as consumers. On the supply line, schools are viewed as closed or open. The four quadrants from these two dimensions combined are labelled the "conservation" scenario (closed + social), "survival" scenario (closed + individual), "transformation" scenario (open + social), and the "market" scenario (open + individual).

*A cross-sectoral typology of scenarios and their uses*

Philip van Notten defines "scenarios" as: "consistent and coherent descriptions of alternative hypothetical futures that reflect different perspectives on past, present, and future developments, which can serve as a basis for action". Many of the studies he reviews were carried out in other sectors – such as in environment, energy, transport, technology, and regional development – and thus are valuable to those in education who may be unfamiliar with them.

He then proposes and discusses in the main part of the chapter a typology of scenario methods. This is divided into three "macro" characteristics – goals, design and content – and ten "micro" characteristics within these broad categories. This typology demonstrates the diversity of scenario approaches and the ways and contexts in which they are used, as well as the outputs they produce.

Van Notten discusses the organisational arrangements which can help make scenario exercises effective, described as "cultures of curiosity", and advocates the value of very long-term thinking.

*Futures studies as a discipline and the "possibility-space" approach to scenarios*

Riel Miller presents the field of futures studies, interest in which is shaped by the speed and complexity of change, and draws a number of parallels with the study of history. He describes the problems with our search after greater predictive accuracy: one is of adopting forecasting methods that depend on extrapolating the past; another is that preoccupation with what is likely can obscure other futures which may appear less likely but which are possible and potentially more desirable. Scenarios have the potential to overcome some of the pitfalls of predictive approaches and hence can be a valuable tool for strategic thinking.

Scenarios based on the modelling of trends or of clarifying visions – "trends-based" and "preference-based" scenarios – may sometimes share similar limitations as predictive approaches and so constrain "out-of-the-box" thinking. Miller presents the "possibility-space" approach as an alternative which builds scenarios through steps: determining or defining the key attribute of the scenario's subject; sketching a space using the primary attributes of change of that attribute; and identifying distinct scenarios within the defined possibility space.

*Successful scenario processes –*
*guidelines for users*

This chapter by Jonas Svava Iversen gives a user-oriented view of a range of scenario methodologies. He presents scenario methods in terms of four critical phases, giving insights about successful practice and potential pitfalls:

- *Mapping and delineation* of the subject matter is a critical first step – giving focus and helping to ensure good design.

- *Identification of critical issues and trends*: analysis may draw from different scientific fields and the participation of experts to provide insights and new perspectives.

- *Creating scenarios.* Iversen sub-divides this core part of the chapter into five: i) identification of drivers; ii) consolidation of trends; iii) prioritisation of trends; iv) identification of scenario axes; and v) actor analysis.

- *Using scenarios* looks at three main uses – developing shared knowledge, strengthening public discourse, and as a tool to support decisions –, commenting on the contexts when these arise and some of the best ways of achieving them.

Iversen concludes by stressing the importance of creating ownership and making sure that scenario procedures are clear for all participants; he argues for a broadly-based and inclusive approach.

## 2. Futures thinking in action

Part Two presents examples from initiatives in England, the Netherlands, New Zealand and Ontario, Canada, which have used scenarios in practice to address on-going reform agendas. It concludes with insights for the future from leading experts on the basis of these initiatives.

*Using scenarios to build leadership capacity – the English FutureSight project*

FutureSight is a multi-partnership English initiative developed with OECD. The purpose has been to build capacity for futures thinking through practical applications to help school leaders shape, not just guess at, the future. It has been used with leaders from schools in very different circumstances, senior organisation officers, older secondary students, and senior policy makers. The chapter describes both the tool itself and how it was developed and used. It is based on a four-module cycle, which:

- Explores key trends and sees where they might go ("a stone rolling").

- Experiences the scenarios from different perspectives ("making it real").

- Gives tools to analyse and reach consensus over an ideal composite scenario ("towards a preferred future").

- Compares current practice and policy and the ideal ("re-engaging with the present").

The discussion reports detailed feedback given by the participants to the FutureSight experience.

*Futures thinking as an arm of decentralised innovation in the Netherlands*

The Dutch government's educational steering philosophy combines decentralisation and more autonomy for schools, with a greater influence for stakeholders. There are multi-year policy plans giving a vision for each sector of education, both in the short term (four years) and the longer term (eight to ten years). Two initiatives have featured in the OECD "Schooling for Tomorrow" programme.

One is about capacity building for visionary leadership through the events on futures thinking organised by the Dutch Principals Academy. Scenarios similar to those in Ontario (Chapter 10) have been used with mixed groups of primary school leaders to stimulate creative thinking, and to address fundamental questions about school design: Why should one learn? What does one have to learn? Where and how can one learn? How can learning be organised? How can learning be supported in the future?

The second project focuses on one example of a radical innovation in schooling – Slash/21 – which rests on a particular vision of the future, with two core concepts: the rise of the knowledge society and increasing individualisation.

*System-wide rethinking of schooling – the New Zealand Secondary Futures programme*

The New Zealand Secondary Futures initiative is working towards a vision for secondary education by: *creating space* to contemplate the future; *providing tools* to resource thinking about the future; *sharing trends* for the future direction of New Zealand society; *sharing information* about possibilities to make more students more successful; *eliciting people's preferences* in relation to the future of the education system; *supporting change* by taking information out to others. This initiative has taken a unique approach to protecting the independence of the process by appointing four "guardians" with high profiles in the educational and non-educational fields.

The themes and key questions emerging from Secondary Futures have been combined into a matrix which provides the structure for ongoing conversations, investigations and analysis. The matrix also serves as a virtual filing cabinet – an online repository for information gathered during the course of the Secondary Futures events and as a reservoir of stimulus material to sustain educational rethinking.

*Creating dialogue and capacity to rethink "Teaching as a Profession" in Ontario*

In the English-speaking school system in Ontario, the "Teaching as a Profession" initiative developed and adapted scenario tools for a series of workshops. The background was a tense period when consensus had been difficult and the initial task was to use scenarios to help forge dialogue on a key policy issue.

The Ontario project uses a multiple-scenario strategic planning framework which identifies desirable futures and the strategies for achieving them. It has used modified OECD scenarios, now relabelled Redefining the Past, Breakdown, the Community-focused Model, Macro Models, and Breakthroughs in Complexity Science. The project has engaged an increasingly wide variety of experts, teachers and others to clarify how alternative ideas about schools and schooling will have consequences for teaching as a profession. It is expected to lead to the identification of preferred scenarios together with robust strategies to further policy discussion and decision-making.

*The "seventh scenario" for the future of Ontario francophone schooling –*
Vision 2020

The *Vision 2020* initiative has proved to be timely given that Ontario's francophones had gained access to school governance at the end of the 1990s yet amidst concern about assimilation and the erosion of their unique culture. The Ministry, French-language educational institutions, and the various partners in education, felt the need to assess their progress, define the challenges they face in delivering quality French-language education, and reflect on the future of French-language education in Ontario.

The scenario-based approach to visualising the parameters of the school of tomorrow has proved valuable as a means to develop the capacity to think about the future. From a starting point of the OECD six schooling scenarios, this initiative has worked towards its own seventh scenario of the future of French-language schooling. The *Vision 2020* project will not conclude before the end of 2006, but it is expected to lead to the development of an operational vision for French-language schooling as a minority system.

*Leading thinkers reflect on the practice and potential for education of futures thinking*

The rapporteurs of the June 2004 Toronto Forum were called upon both to advance general priorities for futures thinking in education and to comment on the particular volunteer system they had followed. Their contributions show how much store they place in the potential of the futures thinking approach but they are also struck by the complexity of educational change.

Charles Ungerleider focuses particularly on value questions – the ways of using futures thinking to clarify those values at stake and the relations, including conflicts, between them. Raymond Daigle asks whether much current reform is often "tinkering at the edges", so that scenarios might help in more fundamental re-definitions. Walo Hutmacher argues the need to consolidate the evidence base for such approaches, and to use robust analytical tools rather than move quickly to normative debate.

Hanne Shapiro echoes these positions and calls for the scope of futures thinking stakeholders and methodologies to be broadened. Tom Bentley distinguishes between and discusses the "inward-facing" and "outward-facing" aspects to futures thinking in action. He considers how scenarios can help trigger different thinking but that this is a particular challenge as regards policy makers themselves, who need both futures analysis that is robust and relevant and need to engage in a setting which enables them to be candid and open-minded about their existing commitments.

# Part One

# Creating and Using Scenarios to Make a Difference in Education

# Chapter 1
# Education in the information age: scenarios, equity and equality

by
Jay Ogilvy[1]

*Jay Ogilvy addresses here the application of scenario planning to the future of education. He first reflects on methods and the different uses of scenarios, comparing features of education and business. He then illustrates the methodological points. He shows how parallels can be drawn between the challenges facing school decision-making and those of "precision farming", using sophisticated personalised approaches. Jay Ogilvy calls for a much more sustained realisation of equity and equality as essential in the Information Age when access to knowledge is fundamental. And, he argues for applying market principles as opposed to the excessive bureaucracy that can stifle educational innovation.*

## Implementing scenario planning

The teams working with the OECD "Schooling for Tomorrow" project from different countries are enthusiastic about the use of scenarios in general, and grateful for the hard work, solid research, and creative insight that informed the OECD/CERI scenarios. But each found it necessary to customise the scenarios in some way in order to get buy in from their own local constituencies. This is a common problem. At Global Business

---

[1] Co-founder of Global Business Network and partner of the Monitor Group.

Network (GBN) we have a saying: "Scenarios are a little like sex – talking about other people's is never as interesting as your own."

In propagating the use of scenarios we face a dilemma: if you supply ready-made scenarios, buy-in and ownership can pose a problem. But if you expect each nation, each district, each school site to create its own customised scenarios, you may lack the resources to provide skilled facilitation, research, and the time necessary to do the job right. There is a way through this dilemma. Very briefly, the solution is to provide a scenario "starter kit" as part of a "toolbox"; the question then is just how much or how little to put in it. To answer this question, it helps to look at three different uses of scenarios: to provoke strategic conversation; to stimulate genuinely new, visionary thinking; and as a motivator for getting unstuck.

## *Scenarios as tools to provoke strategic conversation*

One of the main benefits of scenarios is their capacity to engage participants in a process of civil conversation about the future of education. A set of alternative scenarios provides a very broad tent under which people with widely differing, and often passionately held, views can speak with one another about their children's future. Because scenarios are "just stories", and not yet plans cast in concrete, they can be entertained and discussed in a realm well short of dedicated commitment. Because scenarios are divergent, because they do not, at first, force convergence on consensus, they allow widely different views go gain a respectful hearing. For this reason, they are good tools for engaging an entire community, or an entire nation. Scenario planning is a safe game for consenting adults where you do not get blood on the walls.

This positive feature of scenario planning has its downside for educators, however. Where business people tend to be action oriented, educators tend to be talk oriented. When conducting scenario planning in a business context, it is often difficult to get entrepreneurial managers to have the patience needed to develop a set of scenarios about different possible environments without leaping ahead toward actions to be taken this coming Monday. Business people do not want to talk about what their world may do to them; they want to talk about what they can do to their world. They do not want to take the kind of "outside-in" perspective characteristic of scenario planning; they want to take the kind of "inside-out" perspective – the activist perspective characteristic of entrepreneurs.

Having worked both sides of the street – in education policy and in business – I suggest that scenario planners in education need to be cognisant of these tendencies. It is important to be aware of educators' preference for talk over action. Faced with strategic choices, educators are inclined to ask for further research and more deliberation where business people will opt for immediate action. As business consultant, Tom Peters, has put it: "Ready, fire, aim!" Educators want to aim, and aim carefully, before they fire. They want to think first – for good reason – and act later, sometimes so much later that action never quite happens.

Scenario planners in education need thus to make sure that the scenarios do not become pretexts for endless conversations. They need to make sure that the scenarios *get used to make decisions*. To that end, they need to make sure that those who are capable of making and implementing decisions take ownership of whatever ready-made scenarios are placed in front of them. And for that purpose, one of the best methods is to engage participants in a participatory exercise that *uses and enhances* the scenarios without necessarily disassembling and reassembling them.

In GBN experience, one of the best such exercises is the development of lists of *early indicators*. This exercise has a dual function: first, the process of brainstorming early indicators for each scenario requires an immersion in the content and logic of each scenario. As people try to imagine the first signs of a given scenario, they inevitably find themselves imaginatively occupying the world described by that scenario. Once so engaged, and once they find themselves contributing early indicators, they are more likely to take ownership of the scenarios. Where this first function may be a covert result of the *process* of engagement, the second function is providing the overt product – the lists of early indicators. As the second half of this paper will argue in greater detail, early indicators – of scenarios, and of the success or failure of schools or individual students – are much more to be desired than trailing indicators when remediation is inevitably too late.

So to summarise this first methodological point about the uses of scenarios: the good news – their divergence allows different views a respectful hearing; the bad news – educators may listen and talk for ever without acting. So make sure that people *engage* with the scenarios and use them to make and implement decisions. And to that end, engage them in the process of developing lists of early indicators.

## *Scenarios can stimulate new, visionary thinking*

Just as we tend to parent the way we were parented, so we tend to educate the way we were educated. It is not easy to imagine genuinely new ways to do something so utterly familiar to all of us. So fundamental a feature of the human experience is about as subject to innovation as eating or sleeping. But we *have* changed our eating habits. Improved nutrition has extended life expectancy. Surely we should be able to imagine better ways to educate.

Part of the challenge lies not only in the inertia of fixed habits but in the systematic interconnections among the many parts of our educational systems. As systems theorists are wont to say, *you can't change just one thing.* Try to change one aspect of the curriculum – *e.g.*, class size – and you upset other parts of the system. In California, Governor Pete Wilson surprised both the citizens and the teachers' union with a reduced class size initiative. What a wonderful idea! We all knew that young children were not getting enough individualised attention in large classes. But what seemed like a good idea at the time had not been thought through. Had there been detailed scenarios, the Governor might have seen the consequences of the consequences, namely, that smaller classes would require more teachers and more classrooms. As it happened, the initiative resulted in a sharp increase in the number of inner-city children learning in makeshift trailers from hastily recruited and non-credentialed "teachers". What seemed like a good idea at the time ran the danger of increasing, not decreasing, the inequality between poor inner-city schools and rich suburban schools.

Scenarios, just because they are whole stories and not analytic theories, can provide a format for entertaining systemic change. Well short of pie-in-the-sky utopian thinking, positive scenarios can depict the interactions among the many, many parts of the education *system:* teachers, students, buildings, parents, the local community, new technology, the school-to-work transition, economics, etc. There is no single silver bullet for educational reform, and no one reform is likely to survive unless it is connected up with other parts of a *new* system that will support it. Change just one thing, and the rest of the system will pull that reform back into the old equilibrium, as many reformers have discovered. But in order to change everything at once, you need the kind of holistic, comprehensive vision that a positive scenario can provide.

Because systemic reform is so challenging, positive scenarios are intellectually very difficult to craft. Negative scenarios are much easier – you just describe the demise of what you already know. But positive scenarios must paint something new, a reality as yet unseen. For this reason, positive scenarios run the risk of rejection for being too optimistic, too utopian. Just as it is difficult to anticipate technological breakthroughs – who knew they needed a Xerox machine before it was invented – so it is difficult to anticipate what a better school would look like. But unless we are prepared to believe that the schools we have are the best we *could* have, we have to believe that the breakthroughs are out there, just beyond the horizon of habit and familiarity. And scenarios are the tools for stimulating us to imagine those holistic, comprehensive, systemic reforms that go beyond silver bullet solutions.

In keeping with the methodological hint about using early indicators to engage audiences in scenarios they did not invent themselves, here is a hard won hint for shaping positive scenarios in a way that will enhance their acceptability: let them be short, not long; sketchy, not detailed. In his book, Stephen Denning (2000) advocates what he calls a "minimalist" style of story-telling – brief vignettes that purposely leave a lot to the listener's own imagination. Precisely by leaving a lot of space for the reader or listener to fill in for him or herself, minimalist stories enhance the likelihood that they will take ownership of a story to which they have contributed.

Minimalist storytelling also manages a marriage of convenience with the main challenge of positive scenarios: smarter minds than ours have tried to invent a better education, and they have not succeeded yet. This is a *hard* problem. If we had solved it already, we would already be in that more positive scenario. The fact that we *need* school reform is itself evidence that we lack the solutions we need to give a detailed description to a more positive scenario. So for that reason as well, best to leave the positive scenarios somewhat sketchy. Paint the allure, but leave a veil of unknowing. Precisely in order to seduce, do not try to show it all.

## *Scenarios as a motivator for getting unstuck*

The methodological advice is precisely opposite in the case of negative scenarios. Muster all the production values at your disposal to paint worst case scenarios that are so ugly they function like morality plays: the movie, *The Day After Tomorrow,* does not claim to be great science but the special effects people in Hollywood and their portrait of New York under ice may have done more to stimulate broad concern about carbon-dioxide and rapid climate change than any number of scholarly discourses on the subject. Doom-and-gloom scenarios are psychologically difficult. We do not like worst case scenarios, even in our imagination. But, again, they are intellectually easy to draw. You do not have to invent a *better* way; you just have to destroy the existing way. By rehearsing the disaster in imagination, you may avoid it in reality. Negative scenarios drawn in all their gory detail can deliver a kind of *anticipatory disaster relief.* They can motivate the lethargic masses by putting the fear of God – or the hell of the worst case scenario – into them.

It is not hard to imagine bad scenarios for education. In *Savage Inequalities,* Jonathan Kozol describes schools so decrepit and classrooms so hopeless it is frightening. The second part of this chapter is therefore devoted to the issue of educational inequality, and what it might take to reduce it. While not cast in the form of a scenario – it is not a story with a beginning, middle, and an end – it nonetheless illustrates some of the methodological points I have just made. Though far short of a systemic solution to educational reform, it provides a minimal sketch for improvement by way of an extended analogy between what I call "precision schooling", and the already existing practice of precision farming. It is just a sketch, but it highlights the importance of early indicators, and the promise of new information technologies.

## A declaration of educational equality

Over two centuries ago, America's *Declaration of Independence* stated, "All men are created equal". Women, unfortunately, had to wait over a century before they received the vote, and some women are waiting still for full respect of their humanity. And people of colour continue to fight racism and the legacies of disadvantage. Over a century ago the United States fought its only civil war to put an end to slavery. During the 1960s the civil rights movement, led by the likes of Martin Luther King Jr., sacrificed more lives to bring an end to segregation in our schools. The idea of "separate but equal" education did not deliver on the promise of equal rights to "life, liberty, and the pursuit of happiness".

The noble quest to honour the dignity of *all* citizens is being tested once again. For many reasons – from the invention of the automobile and the advent of the suburbs to the information revolution and the globalisation of the job market – we now find ourselves in a situation where people of colour are not receiving the equal rights granted to them under the laws of most OECD countries. Nor are the poor in developing nations around the globe receiving the kind of schooling that would help lift them out of poverty.

Call the problem the crisis of urban education in the advanced nations, or – following Manuel Castells's (1998, in particular Chapter 2) description of pockets of poverty in both advanced and developing worlds in the new, globalised information economy – call it the crisis of the "black holes of informational capitalism". In fact it is most sorely felt as a crisis for people of colour. During the last half of the $20^{th}$ century, white flight from the centres of many major cities left minorities in old and run down schools while many of the mostly white children attended newer and better staffed schools in the suburban cities. In principle, the U.S. ended segregation with the Civil Rights Act of 1964 and Supreme Court decisions like *Brown vs. the Board of Education*. But *de facto,* segregation is still with us. The facts are overwhelming and irrefutable. When you compare the educational performance of inner city children with suburban children, you find an intolerable gap in achievement.

This gap is morally intolerable. We are all the worse if some of us are denied the tools they need to pursue life, liberty and happiness. This gap is also economically intolerable. The benefits of the information revolution and the knowledge economy extend mainly to those who have the knowledge to use information to their own and others' benefit. In the information age, in what some call the knowledge economy, we are all worse off if some of us cannot read or write. We are all worse off if some of us cannot solve the simple tasks of reading a bus schedule or writing a cheque. We are all worse off if some of us cannot cope with more complex tasks like filling out the forms to manage our own health or the health of our families. Educational inequity is everybody's problem. We all have much to gain – or much to lose – depending on how well we address what Jonathan Kozol calls *Savage Inequalities*. You cannot blame parents, black or white, for moving to the suburbs to find better schools for their children. And you cannot blame minorities for poor academic achievement in schools that their classmates abandoned for good reason. But you can and should expect the citizens of the OECD nations to tackle a problem which, left unsolved, will hurt all of us.

We must come to grips with educational inequity – boldly, intelligently, and with the courage of our convictions. Almost 40 years ago President Lyndon Johnson declared a "War on Poverty". Institutions like the World Bank, the IMF and the OECD have been fighting this war around the world. We have not won this war, in part because we mistook the real enemy. In a knowledge economy, the only way you can win the war on poverty is to wage war on ignorance. We can finally win the war on poverty if, first, we win the war on ignorance. But in order to win the war on ignorance, we need to address the black holes of informational capitalism in developing nations and in the urban ghettoes of OECD countries.

How will we go about solving the problems of educational inequity and *de facto* segregation? And what should the role of federal governments be in providing a solution? The first step consists in recognising the seriousness of the problem. The second consists in gaining clarity about its origins and causes. Our public schools bear the scars of their birth in the agricultural and industrial eras. Schools get long summer vacations because, when our public school system was first founded, students were expected to spend their summers tending animals and harvesting crops. The industrial revolution also left its marks on our schools. During the first half of the $20^{th}$ century there was a major change in the way we educated our children. Educators were deeply influenced by the lessons of scientific management that allowed the industrial revolution to lift so many out of poverty. Henry Ford introduced methods of mass manufacturing for the mass market of America's increasing middle class. Where craftsmen in the $19^{th}$ century hand-crafted carriages one by one for an elite clientele, Henry Ford invented the assembly line to mass-manufacture identical Model-Ts at a price his workers could afford. The cars were cheap because they were produced by the tens of thousands. Mass manufacturing relied on economies of scale.

Scientific management and the industrial revolution were great achievements that helped to build the economies of the OECD. No wonder our educators wanted to model schools after factories. The scientific progressives of the early 20$^{th}$ century achieved economies of scale in education by creating large schools to replace the one room school houses. Students were seated in rows as rational and orderly as the factory floor. In the name of equity, they were given identical lessons in lock-step sequences modelled on the assembly line (Senge, 2000). Industrial age education worked after a fashion. High school graduation rates increased many-fold in OECD nations between 1900 and 1960.

But that was the industrial era improving on the one room school houses of the agricultural era. Now we are heirs to an information revolution every bit as important as the industrial revolution. But we have not yet updated our schools according to the lessons of the information revolution. Industry now uses the fruits of the information revolution to achieve efficiencies without resorting to economies of scale. Rather than relying on mass markets that want more and more of the same, new methods of manufacturing use computers to customise different products for different customers.

## From precision farming to precision schooling

Not just industrialists but farmers as well are using the fruits of the information revolution to improve their yields. In the past ten years, information technology has come to agriculture under the name "precision farming". Farmers use satellite imagery to spot patterns on their fields, sensors on the ground to test for moisture, and global positioning satellites (GPS) and onboard computers to customise the distribution of seeds, water, herbicides and fertilizers foot by foot as their combines cross their fields.

Some information is gathered at harvest time. Equipped with GPS, a combine can pick and weigh a crop and record the information as it crosses a field. (Think of outcomes, standards, and accountability as analogues.) This information is then used when the field is next tilled, planted, treated and fertilized. Sensors on the ground and satellite imagery also gather information on soil quality and moisture. That information, too, can be factored into the application of seeds, herbicides and fertilizers. By knowing what each square foot of field needs, then using that knowledge to administer what is wanted, precision farming moves beyond an industrial paradigm.

Today's most advanced equipment carries the fertilizer elements in separate tanks, both to and in the field, and mixes them just before dispersal. To accomplish this, the farmer must mount a GPS receiver on the fertilizer truck so that the equipment knows its location in the field. An in-vehicle computer must contain the fertilizer-needs maps, which it compares to the field position data arriving from the GPS receiver. It also controls the distribution valves and gates to provide an appropriate fertilizer mix. When everything is working right, the equipment applies the appropriate amount of each fertilizer element to every area (site) in the field. This is where the words "site-specific-farming" were derived ("site-based management" is the educational analogue). Each site in a field is treated uniquely according to its needs. The old industrial paradigm would "mass manufacture" plants using a standardised, uniform distribution of elements. The new paradigm treats each plant site individually, optimising the mix of elements – what is wanted and what is provided – foot by foot. Let us ask, "If we can apply technology to optimise our farming, individual plant by individual plant, then why can't we apply technology to optimising our schooling, individual student by individual student?"

Once upon a time we farmed and we schooled individual by individual. A farmer walking his fields could treat different plants differently depending on an up close appraisal of what each plant needed. The teacher in the one room school house could treat each student individually because she knew them each as individuals. Then the industrial paradigm took over, both in agriculture and in education. Individual-by-individual craftsmanship was inefficient. We started mass manufacturing both plants and students. Industrial agribusiness worked pretty well at increasing crop yields. Mass manufacturing students according to an industrial paradigm was less successful. It seems that students are less responsive to standardised procedures than plants. One size/dose does not fit all, whether we're talking about fertilizer or arithmetic.

The industrial paradigm works with economies of scale: the more widgets you produce using the very same elements and procedures, the lower the cost per widget. Impressed by the economies of scale achieved by industry, our schools and our farms both fell under the influence of the industrial paradigm. But now industry itself, in our new information era, is yielding to what some call "a post-Fordist paradigm". Using computers and programmable robotics, our manufacturing facilities are achieving economies of scale with much shorter runs. They call it "adjustable manufacturing". Levis can be cut to order using information gathered about individual bodies; Benetton can adjust the mix of dyes and colours upstream at its manufacturing facilities depending on the colours that consumers pulled off the shelf on any given day. And now even agriculture is yielding to this post-industrial, information-driven, post-Fordist paradigm. Can education be far behind?

For many decades, education was managed according to inputs: how many teachers? How much seniority did each teacher have? How many hours of in-service training? These were the criteria used to allocate resources and adjust rewards. Now, as in other industries like health care, the attention is shifting from inputs to outputs. In health care we hear of "outcomes research"; in education, we hear of standards and accountability.

What precision farming adds to the picture is a portrait of the way the measurement of outputs can be used in real time: "just before dispersal". It is important to know that one school does better than another at getting its graduates into their first-choice colleges. But how much better it would be if the measurement of outputs could be combined with the detailed, precise measurement of conditions. That way inputs could be adjusted in real time in order to treat each student "uniquely according to his or her needs".

Efforts at farming once fields have failed – once the nutrients have been stripped, or erosion has taken its toll leaving dust or hard-pan – are likewise unfruitful. So, farmers do not wait for fields to fail. They close the cybernetic feedback loop from assessment to intervention in real time, minute by minute, as combines cross fields, foot by foot. School district turnaround consultant, Karen Hawley-Miles writes:

*We already know that most urban schools do not meet state or district performance standards. Student performance is a lagging, not immediate measure of whether schools are providing the kind of instruction that is likely to improve student performance. Estimates of how long it takes to improve test scores range from three to seven years... Reviews of efforts to intervene once schools have failed show that such rescue attempts are unpredictable and expensive. By the time a school has dramatically failed, the cost to turn it around can be high and the time it takes to do so even longer.*

Hawley-Miles suggests the need for *leading* indicators of performance rather than lagging indicators of failure. If we can find leading indicators analogous to the evidence of on-the-ground sensors and satellite imagery, then we will gain the "Ability to act *quickly* to *support* and make necessary *changes* in failing schools."

Let us beware of pushing this analogy too far. Children are not vegetables. Hence Hawley-Miles cautions: "The idea of measuring leading indicators of instructional improvement does not suggest mandating a particular curriculum, instructional approach or way of organising schools." Even if we had better measures of success or failure, school by school or student by student, it is not clear that we know what to do with that data. We probably know more about what it takes to grow asparagus under different conditions than we know about what it takes to grow young minds under different conditions. We lack the educational equivalent of a precisely articulated formula for balancing the mix of nutrients needed for maximum plant growth because human beings are far more complex than artichokes. And so much the better!

As we made the transition from the agricultural era to the industrial era, one of the main missions of the public education system – in the United States at least – was to *socialise* children from many different backgrounds. As rural families came down off the farms to find jobs in cities, and as immigrant families came to America from different lands, there was a need to offer a common curriculum that would socialise children toward a common experience of shared citizenry. In the information era, the job of socialisation is largely accomplished by the media. The first signs of this functionality of the media came when families huddled around their radios to hear the first national broadcasts; today, the media beam American culture worldwide. The job of shared socialisation is being accomplished all-too-well for those who would like to protect indigenous cultures.

But this does have its positive impact for it means that the mission of public education can shift: from industrial era standardisation to information era customisation. Like information era farmers, information era educators can afford to treat each student differently, and the differences that make a difference are not only differences in age, income, and ability – analogous to plant heights and irrigation needs – *but also differences in learning style.* As a result of the pioneering work of Harvard psychologist, Howard Gardner, we now have a cogent theory, and an increasing body of evidence, to support the idea that simple measures like IQ as measured by Alfred Binet need to be supplemented by subtler diagnostics on at least seven different types of intelligence – linguistic, musical, logical-mathematical, spatial, bodily-kinaesthetic, inter-personal, and intra-personal intelligence (Gardner, 1985). Skilled teachers have always recognised that some students learn better by listening, others by reading, still others by acting out new ideas with their whole bodies. Now we have a theory that allows us to diagnose and systematise these different aptitudes.

In the future, there is every reason to believe that we will have learning tools that will allow us to diagnose each individual student in ways that will permit us to treat each student, individually, every hour of every day, with just those educational tools and lesson plans best suited to his or her needs and aptitudes. We will have interactive educational computer games that will automatically diagnose each player's learning style. Such software will accommodate itself not only to so-called "self-paced learning"; it will also permit self-styled learning.

With due respect to the differences between growing minds and growing plants, the force of the precision farming analogy is to underline the fact that we are currently acting as if we do have the formula for raising minds, and it is *one size fits all*. Much of the rhetoric of the standards movement pushes toward industrial era standardisation. The power of the precision farming analogy is to stress the need for more accurate early indicators and assessment tools in order to make non-standard adjustments – granting the fact that we still lack a precisely articulated formula for adjusting our "nutrients" once we have better assessments. (Two recent OECD/CERI publications discuss these questions in detail; one [2006] on personalising education; the other [2005] on formative assessment.)

Another aspect of precision farming might also suggest limits on how far we can push the analogy to precision schooling. When yield-mapping technology first emerged, many thought the goal would be to produce a uniformly high yield. However, the cost of such an approach (both in real dollars and in environmental impact) may lead toward a system that attempts to optimise yield in relation to profit. We may find that some areas should not be farmed. In fact, precision farming may cause farmers to adopt practices that produce even more yield variability than they initially found in the fields. It makes sense to *optimise* rather than maximise or equalise. But educators committed to equity should not be willing to write off a single school or a single student.

Granting such limitations to the analogy, however, it is precisely the distinction between equity and equality that calls for careful assessment of leading indicators and quick interventions. "Equality" can be legislated, and equal dollars per student may flow to different schools. But a closer look at the differing needs of different students – special education, bilingual education, students at risk, and different learning styles for different types of intelligence – shows that the industrial standardisation of "equality" is not adequate. In place of industrial standardisation, we need a more organic understanding of different needs and how to satisfy them. And for that understanding, we could do worse than take a few lessons from the analogy with precision farming. If farmers can grow cornstalks one by one using information to customise their nutrients one stalk at a time, isn't it time that we educate our children one by one, one student at a time?

Equity in education is not achieved by pumping the same inputs into every school. An information age approach to schooling can close the gap by treating each school, each student, differently as needs require. You use information technology to identify particular needs, and then you meet those needs by using information technology to administer different "nutrients" affordably. Skilled teachers have always known that each child is unique, and they have done their best to teach one student at a time. But skilled teachers have been fighting uphill against over-crowded, factory-like classrooms and assembly-line lesson plans. In order to achieve educational equity in the information era, we need to make a break from the old industrial-era model of mass-manufacturing well-socialised, identical students. We need to gather information about each district, each school, each student, and use that information to adjust the levels of "nutrients" – whether dollars, or teachers, or text books, or computers – as each school, each student requires. As the example of precision farming shows, this is an affordable, attainable dream in the information age.

We have already begun to gather some of the information we need. This is what the educational standards movement is all about – finding out who is doing well and who is not. But the standards movement, at least as it is currently being practiced in the United States, is out of step with the information revolution. It is entirely too focused on standardisation – as if the federal government were trying to tell each and every state and school district how to run its schools. Educational standards could be used to gather information to treat different schools differently in order to achieve educational equity. But, the standards movement has become a stick with which to punish under-performing schools, not a diagnostic tool to enhance the education of individual students. Just as the farmers need those geographic positioning satellites looking over everybody, so we need some national standards as tools of measurement. But we must use that information to differentiate: to customise the spread of nutrients, not to impose some uniform solution.

## Differences that make a difference

If our first principle for reform is educational equity, then our second principle, derived from the difference between the industrial era and the information era, is that equity calls for differences that make a difference, not just a uniform spread of the same standardised inputs. A third principle that should guide our retooling of education for the information era is the role of market forces when it comes to spreading valuable resources. Government still has a job to do but it has more to do with assuring that markets operate fairly and properly.

How might market mechanisms apply to public education? School boards and district central offices operate like state monopolies. Parents and students have no other choice of provider, as they would in a free market. In most businesses a manager can make changes to accommodate the different needs of different customers. But after decades of tough negotiations between school boards and teachers' unions, the public education system, in the U.S. at least, has become hog-tied by hundreds of agreements which forbid teachers and principals from making the changes needed by students. The American public education system is not so much broken as it is locked – frozen into immobility by miles of print in volumes of code sitting on yards of shelves in every state capital. We must unlock this system if we are to unleash the innovation we need to educate our children for the Information Age.

Let's not blame the unions for defending the interests of underpaid teachers. Let's not blame the school boards or superintendents or their staffs in those much maligned central offices. These are for the most part good people trying to do the best job they can. But the game has been rigged in such a way that the harder you play, the more you lose. Teachers lose when the rules will not allow them to be rewarded for jobs well done. School administrators lose when the rules won't allow them the flexibility they need to make improvements. And worst of all, students lose when locked into obsolete, industrial assembly lines that give them no choice among schools or teachers.

We must cut through this educational gridlock and create the rules for a better game, one where students win and teachers and administrators win as well. How to do it? First, we can use the information we are gathering from standard tests and other more subtle diagnostic tools to identify the needs of each student, each school, and each district. Second, we can allow each school to purchase the supplies, the skills, the personnel it needs to satisfy the needs of its students. Because the information we gather will show that some students have special needs, schools should be allocated special funds to meet those special needs. Third, students and their parents can be given the opportunity to shop around for the schools and teachers that best meet their needs. Funding should follow the flow of student choices. Schools that are chosen by unusually high numbers of students with special needs will be given correspondingly larger budgets. Those budgets can be spent on increased salaries for those unusually gifted and heroic teachers who can succeed with students at risk.

A system like this will allow market mechanisms to allocate valuable resources far more equitably than the system now in place. Market forces will reward results – outcomes rather than inputs. Our current system rewards inputs – years of service, courses taken, credentials – rather than proven effectiveness of teachers or schools. The genius of the market is precisely to process information: information about needs and preferences that a monopoly can afford to neglect.

Clearly, markets have their limits. We now know better than to push for the privatisation of everything. Market mechanisms tend to produce winners and losers. Wherever there is a social mandate for universal service – *e.g.*, for communications systems, national security, health care, *and education* – there is a role for governments to play in compensating for market imperfections. But an abiding role for government should not fool us into thinking that centrally planned education monopolies are superior to a combination of market mechanisms and governmental oversight. We should be prepared to pay much more for good teachers than we pay them today. Good teachers deserve to be compensated like other skilled professionals. But we will not be able to free up the funds to reward those good teachers until we break the rule-bound bureaucratic gridlock of most current systems.

If we are going to pay more to those teachers who step in to close the gap between inner-city students and others, where are we going to get the money? A fourth principle says that *urban education is a national crisis that national governments must address.* Our largest cities are national cities, not just the prides of different states or provinces. Some have even called them global cities (Sassen, 1991). New York and London are the financial capitals of the world. Paris and Milan are the fashion capitals of the world. The San Francisco Bay Area is the global capital of the Internet. Sydney and Brisbane serve many needs throughout Southeast Asia. It would be wrong to expect local districts to shoulder by themselves the costs of closing the gaps in their urban schools. This is a job for federal governments.

Still, education is a local responsibility because young children need to sleep in their own beds at night, close to their parents and their local jobs. Unlike manufactured goods that can travel from low cost producers to consumers around the world, schools are as geographically rooted as corn stalks. Children should go to schools in their own neighbourhoods. Like good managers of successful businesses, local school boards should have the ability to make decisions about the allocation of precious resources. The reforms we need will not take the form of some single cookie-cutter plan imposed on all states, all provinces, and all school districts. Quite to the contrary, by introducing market forces into the system, we can allow different districts to purchase the resources they need to meet the different needs of the students they know best. But you cannot send someone to market with no money and then expect market mechanisms to work fairly.

The way the US system is now operating, urban districts are at a disadvantage and a number of states have declared their current educational funding systems unconstitutional because they fail to deliver on the constitutional promise to educational equity. We must right this wrong, but not by taking money away from some to compensate others. Left to their own devices, different states could achieve equity only by redistribution –

levelling to the middle, taking from the privileged to compensate the underprivileged. Because educational equity is a national if not a global problem, federal governments need to get involved to level the playing field by "levelling up" – by giving extra funds to urban districts so that they can come to market with the funds they need.

To summarise the principles that will guide us going forward:

- First, there is equity as the equal right to life, liberty, and the pursuit of happiness which, in the information age, demands an end to ignorance.

- Second, in this information era, equity calls for *differences that make a difference*, not just a uniform spread of the same standardised inputs.

- Third, market mechanisms must supplement down-from-the top bureaucracy when it comes to allocating different resources to different local needs.

- Fourth, while education is a local responsibility, central governments have a job to do to make sure that urban districts have the funds they need to level up.

Putting these principles into practice is a big job. It calls for leadership and local support. We all have a lot to gain – students, teachers, school administrators, parents, and employers – if we can break the deadlock we have inherited from our agricultural and industrial models of education and recognise we now live in an information era with a knowledge economy.

# *References*

Castells, M. (1998), *The Information Age, Vol. III: End of Millennium,* Blackwell Publishers, Cambridge University Press, Cambridge.

Clark, R.L. (1997), "Practices and Potential: Assessing an Agricultural Revolution in Progress", University of Georgia.

Denning, S. (2000), *The Springboard: How Storytelling Ignites Action in Knowledge-Era Organizations,* Butterworth Heinemann, Boston.

Gardner, H. (1985), *Frames of Mind: The Theory of Multiple Intelligences*, Basic Books, New York.

Gardner, H. (1999), *Intelligence Reframed: Multiple Intelligences for the 21$^{st}$ Century*, Basic Books, New York.

Hawley-Miles, K. (2001), "What 'Equity' Means for Urban District Design", Annenberg Task Force on the Future of Urban Districts, The Annenberg Institute for School Reform.

Kozol, J. (1991), *Savage Inequalities*, Crown Publishers, New York.

OECD (2006), *Personalising Education – Schooling for Tomorrow*, OECD, Paris.

OECD (2005), *Formative Assessment – Improving Learning in Secondary Classrooms*, OECD, Paris.

Sassen, S. (1991), *The Global City,* Princeton University Press.

Senge, P. (2000), "The Industrial Age System of Education", in P. Senge *et al.*, *Schools that Learn,* Doubleday, New York, pp. 27-58.

# Chapter 2
# System thinking, system thinkers and sustainability

by
Michael Fullan[1]

*Michael Fullan advises that thinking about the future is not enough for decision makers in education; it is also necessary to conceptualise how to change current systems in specific, powerful ways. He identifies three priority areas to consider: i) the challenge of change, ii) systems thinking, and iii) sustainability as the route to the future. Under the latter, Fullan presents a set of key elements including lateral capacity-building through networks, intelligent accountability, deep learning, dual commitment to short- and long-term results, and cyclical energising. The way forward, he suggests, is to put in place more practical system thinkers, who in turn will guide other leaders in the same direction.*

## Change challenges

In recent years, there has been more attention paid to large-scale educational reform. One of the most ambitious examples of reform is England's National Literacy and Numeracy Strategy (NLNS). A multi-year evaluation of NLNS reached two main conclusions (Earl *et al.*, 2003). On the one hand, NLNS was an impressive and huge success. Literacy and numeracy achievement for 11-year-olds increased from just over 60% in 1997, to about 755 in 2002 – all this in 20 000 schools. On the other hand,

---

[1] Professor and Dean of Ontario Institute of Education (OISE) at the University of Toronto, Canada.

the results levelled off in 2001, and have stayed at that level to the present. This plateau effect – which has been seen in other large scale projects involving whole school districts – signifies that the strategies that generated the earlier results were not sustainable in the next phase of reform. A different approach was needed.

Heifetz and Linsky (2002) confirm this conclusion in their distinction between technical problems (still difficult) for which the existing knowledge base is sufficient to address the problem, and adaptive challenges, for which current knowledge is not available to resolve the problem. The main properties of adaptive challenges can be defined as follows:

- The solution is beyond our current repertoire.
- Adaptive work requires difficult learning.
- The people with the problem are the problem and the solution.
- Adaptive work generates disequilibrium and avoidance.
- Adaptive work takes a longer time to work on effectively.

There is no doubt that the OECD "Schooling for Tomorrow" project represents an adaptive challenge of the highest order. Therefore, it will require new approaches that draw especially on systems and sustainability.

## Systems thinking

Clearly, systems thinking is relevant to changing organisations. This chapter argues that for systems thinking to be practically useful, practitioner-based system thinkers must be developed in action. In this respect the promise of system-thinking has fallen woefully short. No real practical progress has been made in actually promoting systems thinking since Peter Senge (1990) first raised the matter. As Senge laid out the argument:

> *Human endeavours are also systems. They ... are bound by invisible fabrics of interrelated actions, which often take years to fully play out their effects on each other. Since we are part of the lacework ourselves, it is doubly hard to see the whole pattern of change. Instead, we tend to focus on snapshots of isolated parts of the system, and wonder why our deepest problems never seem to get solved. Systems thinking is a conceptual framework, a body of knowledge and tools that has been developed over the past fifty years, to make the full patterns clearer, and* to help us see how to change them effectively. (p. 7, my emphasis)

Recall that systems thinking is the fifth discipline that integrates the other four disciplines: personal mastery, mental models, building shared vision, and team learning. Philosophically, Senge (*op. cit.*, pp. 12-13) is on the right track, but his ideas are not very helpful in practice:

*[Systems thinking] is the discipline that integrates the disciplines, fusing them into a coherent body of theory and practice. It keeps them from being separate gimmicks or the latest organisation fads. Without a systemic orientation, there is no motivation to look at how the disciplines interrelate ...*

*At the heart of a learning organisation is a shift of mind – from seeing ourselves as separate from the world to connected to the world, from seeing problems as caused by someone or something "out there" to seeing how our own actions create the problems we experience. A learning organisation is a place where people are continually discovering how they create their reality and how they can change it.* [my emphasis]

As valid as the argument may be, there is no programme of development that has actually formed leaders to become greater, practical systems thinkers. Until we do this we cannot expect the organisation or system to become transformed. The key to doing this is to link systems thinking with sustainability – defined as the capacity of a system to engage in the complexities of continuous improvement consistent with deep values of human purpose.

## Sustainability

Conceptually the new work of leaders embraces systems thinking *and* sustainability in a way that grounds them practically in local context. The key to moving forward is to enable leaders to experience and become more effective at leading organisations toward greater sustainability.

Fullan (2004) defines eight elements of sustainability:

- Public service with a moral purpose.
- Commitment to changing context at all levels.
- Lateral capacity-building through networks.
- Intelligent accountability and new vertical relationships.
- Deep learning.
- Dual commitment to short-term and long-term results.

- Cyclical energising.
- The long lever of leadership.

In the remainder of this paper, I shall elaborate further on these elements of sustainability.

## Public service with a moral purpose

Moral purpose must transcend the individual to become an organisation and system quality which collectivities are committed to pursuing in all of their core activities (Fullan, 2003b). Moral purpose can be defined in three ways with respect to schools: i) commitment to raising the bar and closing the gap of student achievement; ii) respectful treatment of people without lowering expectations; and iii) orientation to environmental improvement, including other schools in the district. Corporate organisations as well as public institutions must embrace moral purpose if they wish to succeed over the long run.

## Commitment to changing context at all levels

David Hargreaves (2003, p. 74) recalls the observation by Donald Schon, best known for his work on the reflexive practitioner, thirty years ago:

*We must ... become adept at learning. We must become able not only to transform our institutions, in response to changing situations and requirements; we must invest and develop institutions which are "learning systems", that is to say, systems capable of bringing about their own continuing transformation.*

It is not Schon's fault that all these years later this advice remains totally accurate and totally useless. How do you enter the chicken and egg equation of starting down the path of generating learning systems in practice, especially in an era of transparent accountability? This article provides practical response to this question: there is now more powerful evidence that "changing the system" is an essential component of producing learning organisations.

Changing whole systems means changing the entire context within which people work. Researchers are fond of observing that "context is everything" usually in reference to the success of a particular innovation in one situation but not in another. If context is everything, then emphasis must be placed on how it can be changed for the better. This task is not as impossible as it sounds but will take time and cumulative effort. The good news is that once contextual change is underway, it has self-generating powers to go further. Contexts are the structure and cultures within which one works. In the case of educators, the tri-level contexts are school/community, district, and system. The critical question to ask is whether strategies can be identified that will indeed change in a desirable direction the contexts that affect us? Currently these contexts have a neutral or adverse impact on what we do.

On the small scale, Gladwell (2000, pp. 150, 173) has already identified context as a key *Tipping Point*: "the power of context says that what really matters is the little things". If you want to change people's behaviour, "you need to create a community around them, where these new beliefs could be practical, expressed and nurtured". Drawing from complexity theory, I have argued elsewhere that in order to attain system change, the amount of purposeful interaction between and among *individuals* within and across the tri-levels, and indeed within and across *systems* must be increased (Fullan, 2003a).

Therefore, the most essential first step is a commitment to changing context. The remaining six elements of sustainability, which work on a more practical level, follow automatically once the commitment to change has been reached. Commitment to change gives people new experiences, new capacities, and new insights into what should and can be accomplished. It gives people a taste of the power of new context, none more so than the discovery of lateral capacity-building.

## *Lateral capacity-building through networks*

In the past few years, lateral capacity has been discovered as a powerful strategy for school improvement. This discovery was multi-phased. First, greater accountability leading to the realisation that support or capacity-building was essential. This in turn led to vertical capacity-building with external trainers at the district or other levels, which finally led to the realisation that lateral capacity-building across peers was a powerful learning strategy.

A systematic strategy-driven use of networks and collaboratives is evolving in England, partly as a response to the limitations of "informed prescription". Many of the new network strategies are being developed by the National College of Schools Leadership (NCSL). For example, a consultant leaders programme now engages 1 000 of the most effective elementary school principals in the country working with 4 000 other schools. In this one strategy alone, 25% of all school principals in the country are involved in mutual learning.

There are a number of obvious benefits from lateral strategies (see also Hargreaves, 2003). People learn best from peers – fellow travellers who are further down the road – if there is sufficient opportunity for ongoing, purposeful exchange. The system is designed to foster, develop and disseminate innovative practices that work – discoveries that are in the mode of Heifetz and Linsky's adaptive challenges (2002): "solutions that lie outside the current way of operating". Leadership is developed and mobilised in many quarters. At the same time motivation and ownership – a key ingredient for sustainability of effort and engagement – is deepened at the local level.

Lateral capacity, however, is not the only strategy at work but functions in relationship to the other seven elements of sustainability. Complexity theory states that if the amount of purposeful interaction is increased and infused with the checks and balances of quality knowledge, *self-organising* patterns (desirable outcomes) will accrue. This promise is not good enough for the sustainable-seeking society with a sense of urgency. There are at least two problems. One concerns how the issues being investigated can result in disciplined inquiry and innovative results; the other raises the question of how good ideas being generated by networks can be integrated in the line operation of organisations.

## *Intelligent accountability and vertical relationships*

Sustainable societies must solve, *i.e.* hold in dynamic "tension", the perennial change problem of how to attain system-wide local ownership (including capacity) and external accountability at the same time. These problems can only be solved locally:

> *Solutions rely, at least in part, on the users themselves and their capacity to take school responsibility for positive outcomes. In learning, health, work, and even parenting, positive outcomes arise from a combination of personal effort and wider social resources. (Bentley and Wilsdon, 2003, p. 20)*

Yet what will motivate people to seek positive outcomes? Furthermore, how are people and groups to be held accountable for the public or corporate good? The answer is a mixture of collaboration and networks with what David Miliband, the former UK Schools Minister, calls "intelligent accountability". Networks and other professional learning communities (lateral capacity-building) do build in a strong yet incomplete measure of accountability. As such, communities interact to solve given problems in order to generate better practices, shared commitment, and peer accountability. Collaborative cultures are demanding when it comes to results; and the demand is telling because it is peer-based and up close on a daily basis.

At the same time, vertical relationships (state/district, district/school, etc.) must be strengthened not only in terms of support and resources but also accountability. Some of these vertical relationships will come in the form of element five (deep learning) and six (short-term and long-term results). It will be difficult to find the right balance of vertical authority accountability – too much direction demotivates people; too little permits drift or worse. To address this problem, a strategy, "self-evaluation", that has been around for at least 20 years must be reintroduced. In the past, self-evaluation has been touted as an alternative to top-down assessment. In fact, we need to conceive self-evaluation and use it as a both/and solution. Miliband (2004) in a recent speech advocated:

> *An accountability framework, which puts a premium on ensuring effective and ongoing self-evaluation in every school combined with more focused external inspection, linked closely to the improvement cycle of the school... First, we will work with the profession to create a suite of materials that will help schools evaluate themselves honestly. The balance here is between making the process over-prescriptive, and making it just an occasional one-off event. In the best schools it is continuous, searching and objective. Second, [we] will shortly be making proposals on inspection, which take full account of a school's self-evaluation. A critical test of the strong school will be the quality of its self-evaluation and how it is used to raise standards. Third, the Government and its partners at local and national level will increasingly use the information provided by a school's self-evaluation and development plan, alongside inspection, to inform outcomes about targeting support and challenge. (pp. 6, 8)*

Not all systems have a formal inspection agency as in England. However, all systems do have some form of external accountability, which must be reconstituted so that it is too integrated with self-evaluation. And yes, it is extremely difficult to combine self-evaluation and outside evaluation, but herein lies the sophistication of sustainability – for the latter to have a chance, *the whole system* must be involved in a co-dependent partnership that is open to addressing problems as they arise.

## *Deep learning*

Sustainability as defined in this paper requires continuous improvement, adaptation, and collective problem-solving in the face of complex challenges that keep arising. As Heifetz and Linsky (2002) say, adaptive work "demands learning", "demands experimentation", and "difficult conversations". Similarly, "species evolve whereas cultures learn".

There are three major requirements for the data-driven society: drive out fear; set up a system of transparent data-gathering coupled with mechanisms for acting on the data; make sure *all* levels of the system are expected to learn from their experiences. One of Deming's (1986) prescriptions for success was "Drive out Fear". In the *Education Epidemic (2003)*, Hargreaves argues:

> *Government must give active permission to schools to innovate and provide a climate in which failure can be viewed as a necessary element in making progress as is the case in the business world. In other words, mistakes can be accepted or even encouraged, provided that they are a means of improvement. (p. 36)*

Pfeffer and Sutton (2000, pp. 109 and 124-255) devote a whole chapter to "When Fear Prevents Acting on Knowledge": "In organisation after organisation that failed to translate knowledge into action, we saw a pervasive atmosphere of fear and distrust." Significantly, Pfeffer and Sutton identify two other "pernicious effects". One is that "fear causes a focus on the short run [driving] out consideration of the longer run". The other problem is that "fear creates a focus on the individual rather than the collective". In a punitive culture, if I can blame others, or others make a mistake, I am better off. Need I say that both the focus on the short run and excessive individualism are fateful for sustainability?

Second, capacities and means of acting on the data are critical for learning. Thus, "assessment for learning" has become a powerful, high yield tool for school improvement and student learning (see Black *et al.*, 2003). There are two critical aspects of the move toward more effective data use. First, avoid excessive assessment demands (Miliband talks about reducing necessary paper and information burden which distract schools from their core business). Second, ensure that a range of qualitative as well as quantitative data are collected. In discussion of knowledge building in "Leading in a Culture of Change", I cite several examples including the US Army's "After Action Reviews" which have three standardised questions: What was supposed to happen? What happened? And what accounts for the differences? This kind of learning is directed to the future, *i.e.*, to sustainable improvements.

Deep learning means collaborative cultures of inquiry which alter the culture of learning in the organisation away from dysfunctional and non-relationships toward the daily development of culture that can solve difficult or adaptive problems (see especially Kegan and Lahey, 2001; and Perkins, 2003). In a development sense, there is need to train and mentor current and potential future leaders so that they can become proficient at shaping the culture of the organisation in the direction of day-to-day interactions that represent continuous learning.

The "curriculum" for doing this is contained in Kegan and Lahey's seven languages for transformation (*e.g.*, from the language of complaint to the language of commitment), and in Perkins' developmental leadership which represents "progressive interaction" which evokes the exchange of good ideas, and fosters the cohesiveness of the group. These new ways of working involve deep changes in the culture of most organisations, and thus the training and development must be sophisticated and intense.

## *Dual commitment to short-term and long-term results*

Like most aspects of sustainability, things that appear to be mutually exclusive must be brought together. It is a pipedream to argue only for the long-term goal of organisations or society. Shareholders and the public would never permit this. The new reality is that governments and organisations have to show progress in relation to both short- and long-term priorities. Our knowledge base is such that there is no excuse for failing to design and implement strategies that get short-term results.

Of course, short-term progress can be accomplished at the expense of the mid- to long-term (win the battle, lose the war), but they do not have to be. I advocate that organisations set targets and take action to obtain early results and intervene in situations of terrible performance; at the same time, they must invest in the eight sustainability capacity-building elements described in this chapter. Over time, the system grows stronger and fewer severe problems occur as they are pre-empted by corrective action sooner rather than later. Shorter term results are also necessary to build trust with the public or shareholders for longer term investments. Barber (2004) argues that it is necessary to:

> *Create the virtuous circle where public education delivers results, the public gains confidence and is therefore willing to invest through taxation and, as a consequence, the system is able to improve further. It is for this reason that the long-term strategy requires short-term results.*

## *Cyclical energising*

Sustain is derived from the Latin word, *sustineo*, which means "to keep up". However, this definition is misleading for sustainability is not linear. On the contrary, it is cyclical for two fundamental reasons. One has to do with energy, and the other with periodic plateaus where additional time and ingenuity are required for the next adaptive breakthrough. Loehr and Schwartz (2003, pp. 9-14) argue that "energy, not time" is the fundamental currency of high performance. They base their work on four principles:

- *Principle 1*: Full engagement requires four separate but related sources of energy: physical, emotional, mental, and spiritual.

- *Principle 2:* Because energy capacity diminishes both with overuse and under-use, we must balance energy expenditure with intermittent energy renewal.

- *Principle 3:* To build capacity, we must push beyond our normal limits, training in the same systematic way that elite athletes do.

- *Principle 4*: Positive energy rituals – highly specific routines for managing energy – are key to full engagement and sustained high performance.

If we want sustainability we need to keep an eye on energy levels (overuse and under-use). Positive collaborative cultures will help because a) they push for greater accomplishments, and b) they avoid the debilitating effects of negative cultures. It is not hard work that tires us out, as much as it is negative work. In any case, we need combinations of full engagement with colleagues, along with less intensive activities which are associated with replenishment.

There is another reason why sustainability is cyclical. In many cases we have seen achievement in literacy and mathematics improve over a five-year period, only to plateau or level off. It may be related to burnout, but this is not likely the main explanation. People are still putting in a lot of energy to maintain the same higher level performance represented by the new plateau. If people were burning out, performance would likely *decline*.

A more likely explanation is that the set of strategies that brought initial success are not the ones – not powerful enough – to take us to higher levels. In these cases, we would expect the best learning organisations to investigate, learn, experiment, and develop better solutions. *This takes time*. (Incidentally, with the right kind of intelligent accountability we would know whether organisations are engaged in quality problem-solving processes even if their short-term outcomes are not showing increases.) While this new adaptive work is going on, we would not expect achievement scores to rise in a linear fashion, and any external assessment scheme that demanded "annual yearly progress" would be barking up the wrong tree.

Cyclical energising is a powerful new idea. We do not yet have the precision to know what cyclical energising looks like in detail, but the concept needs to be a fundamental element of our sustainability strategies.

## *The long lever of leadership*

If a system is to be mobilised in the direction of sustainability, leadership at all levels of the system must be the primary engine. In this sense the main mark of a great leader at the end of his/her tenure is not his impact on the bottom line but especially how many leaders he/she leaves behind who can progress even further. This work includes helping to put into place all eight elements of sustainability – with all eight feeding on each other. To do this, we need organisations led by people who are trained and developed to think in bigger system terms and to act in ways that affect larger parts of the system.

## Concluding remark

Subsequently, we have been working in partnership with school districts and states to develop an agenda of bringing about system-wide change. We have presented a system solution for achieving "breakthrough" results for 90% or more of students in the basics, such as literacy (Fullan, Hill and Crevola, 2006). My analysis of turnaround intervention strategies from this perspective has found that they at best result in short-term improvements while establishing conditions that virtually guarantee that sustainability cannot result (Fullan, 2006). I have identified what it will take to increase the likelihood of sustainability, using Ontario as a case example.

In sum, we need a new emphasis on system reform which has at its core developing leaders who can take more of a system perspective with a sustainability focus. These I call "system thinkers in action" and there are indeed a number of developments on this front in England and other locations. Such leaders work in turn to develop and support other leaders who can go even further. The agenda for the OECD "Schooling for Tomorrow" project is to establish actual examples of system change and to learn from them to go deeper.

# References

Barber, M. (2004), "Courage and the Lost Art of Bicycle Maintenance", Department for Education and skills, Consultants Conference, London.

Bentley, T. and J. Wilsdon (2003), *The Adaptive State: Strategies for Personalising the Public Realm*, Demos, London.

Black, P., C. Harrison, C. Lee, B. Marshall and D. William (2003), *Assessment for Learning*, Open University Press, Philadelphia.

Deming, W.E. (1986), *Out of the Crisis* (2$^{nd}$ Edition), MIT Cambridge, Mass.

Earl, L. *et al.* (2003), *Watching and Learning 3*, Department for Education and Skills, London.

Fullan, M. (2003a), *Change Forces with a Vengeance*, Routledge Falmer, London.

Fullan, M. (2003b), *The Moral Imperative of School Leadership*, Thousand Oaks, Corwin Press, California/Ontario Principals Council, Toronto.

Fullan, M. (2004), *Leadership and Sustainability*, Thousand Oaks, Corwin Press, California/Ontario Principals Council, Toronto.

Fullan, M. (2006), *Beyond Turnaround Leadership*, Jossey-Bass, San Francisco.

Fullan, M., P. Hill and C. Crevola (2006), *Breakthrough*, Thousand Oaks, Corwin Press, California/Ontario Principals Council, Toronto.

Gladwell, M. (2000), *Tipping Point*, Little Brown, Boston.

Hargreaves, D. (2003), *Education Epidemic*, Demos, London.

Heifetz, R. and M. Linsky (2002), *Leadership on the Line*, Harvard Business School Press, Boston.

Kegan, R. and L. Lahey (2001), *How the Way we Talk can Change the Way we Work*, Jossey Bass, San Francisco.

Loehr, J. and T. Schwartz (2003), *The Power of Full Engagement*, Free Press, New York.

Miliband, D. (2004), "Personalised Learning: Building New Relationships with Schools", speech presented to the North of England Education Conference, Belfast, Northern Ireland, 8$^{th}$ January, 2004.

Mintzberg, H. (2004), *Managers not MBAs*, Berrett-Koehler, San Francisco.

Perkins, D. (2003), *King Arthur's Roundtable*, Wiley, New York.

Pfeffer, J. and R. Sutton (2000), *The Knowing-Doing Gap*, Harvard Business School Press, Boston.

Senge, P. (1990), *The Fifth Discipline: The Art and Practice of Learning*, Doubleday, New York.

# Chapter 3
# Scenarios, international comparisons, and key variables for educational scenario analysis

by
Jean-Michel Saussois[1]

*Jean-Michel Saussois presents basic features of scenarios as ideal types, looking at both the evolution of scenarios and their applications in the business world and their relevance for educational decision-making. He suggests that scenarios involve demanding assumptions which should be understood, especially when the exercise is one of international comparison. The chapter presents a two-dimensional framework within which to analyse the trends and futures for schooling: the shifting values about where schools belong in the social fabric and the delivery or supply function of schooling. These two dimensions are combined to give four new scenarios – conservation, survival, transformation, and market – with discussion of the forces that move educational systems from one to another.*

## Canonic scenarios

The scenario methodology comes from the private sector, mainly developed by large firms dissatisfied with available long-range planning methods. They sought a softer, less quantitative approach incorporating a greater number of assumptions and going so far as to include the insights derived from following hunches. The firms wanted to consider the long run

---

[1] Professor, École supérieure de commerce de Paris-École européenne des affaires (ESCP-EAP).

as descriptions of *possible* futures and also as *desirable* futures *i.e.* those shaped so as to further their own advantage.

A basic scenario approach follows specific steps which can be summed up as follows:

- First: delimitation of the "object" to be observed.
- Second step: identification of key driving variables, both external and internal.
- Third step: matching these variables in a retro-analysis to identify "heavy tendencies" and an analysis of the actual situation to sort out weak signals of change and key actors.
- The fourth step – define strategies of the main actors.
- The fifth step is to propose scenarios…
- …and from these scenarios the final step is to propose action plans.

Among the first large firms to have developed such a scenario methodology was the worldwide oil company Shell during the 1960s, well before the 1974 oil crisis. Shell was one of the first companies to realise the importance of the geo-political dimension; it wanted to shape its environment instead of simply coping with it. In the 1980s, Shell continued using the scenario methodology; it set up, for example, a socio-political forecast study for Europe which identified two scenarios. One was "Europe as a Medieval Castle" resisting liberalism, the other was "Europe as a Common Market" with a governance structure loosely coupled across national levels. The study identified a set of key assumptions which were probabilised in order to identify strategies for the way the corporation could reorganise its European operations. Scenario 2, for example, got right into the question of what it is meaningful to do at the national level. So, the scenario methodology facilitates anticipation and is a tool of governance designed for taking action.

This methodology is not easy to put into practice. The first step of delimiting the object to be observed is often the most difficult – what is the appropriate focus? The corporate level? The firm? The industrial sector? Once the appropriate level is defined, others difficulties arise. The environment such as that for oil which Shell considered can be characterised in terms of the "nested box" or "Russian puppets" problem *i.e.* inside each "box" there is a smaller one. Each one is partly independent of, but constrained by, the shape of those within and outside it and the choice to focus on one specific box (or level) is not a neutral matter.

Establishing key driving forces – what will shape an industry – is not an easy task either. Concerning oil, driving forces can be tax laws, highway expansion, the internal combustion engine, taxes on pollution and so forth. In pharmaceuticals, the big threat for the American industry thirty years ago was the manufacture of drugs under generic names by small competitors (which arose in France only five years or so ago). Then the question raised was: how to react to this threat? Is the American pharmaceutical industry prepared for it? In sum, large firms have used this methodology as a tool for evaluating the future in terms such as the threats which can damage or destroy their interests.

## *Scenarios as ideal types and their use in education*

While there are important differences between the situation facing education policy-making and decision-making in large firms, certain key issues and problems to be addressed are the same. For example, the education system can equally be conceptualised as *a nested box*: the level being addressed is highly relevant to any discussion and analysis, whether it is the school, networks of schools, the school district, the regional education department, the national level, etc. Which one should be the focus is not obvious, and resolving this question is not helped by the confusing term "system". It is also necessary to be clear about whether the focus is on the primary or the secondary school levels because the stakeholders and players involved are not the same in each case.

The OECD "Schooling for Tomorrow" scenarios can be considered as ideal types in the Weberian sense following the sociologist Max Weber (1904, 1946, 1947). He applied this approach to the analysis of bureaucracy and identified eight fundamental categories which characterise a configuration or a set of intertwined dimensions of *rational legal authority:* 1) a continuous organisation of official functions bound by rules; 2) a specified sphere of competence which involves a unit exercising authority as an administrative organ; 3) the organisation of offices follows the principle of hierarchy whereby each lower level is under the control and supervision of the higher one, with a right of appeal and statement of grievance from the lower to the higher; 4) the rules which regulate the conduct of an office may be technical rules and norms – it is thus normally true that only those who have demonstrated an adequate technical training are qualified to be a member of the administration staff and eligible for appointment to an official position; 5) it is a matter of principle that the members of the administration staff should be completely separated from ownership of the means of production; 6) there is an absence of appropriation of their official positions by the incumbents; 7) administrative acts, decisions, and rules are formulated in writing even in cases where oral discussion is the rule; 8) legal authority can be exercised in a wide variety of forms.

Weber's definition of *pure* bureaucracy is an attempt to capture all the forms of organisations relying on rationality rather than tradition, and includes dimensions by which a large private firm or a ministry might be characterised. For instance, such organisations may well be characterised by reliance on expertise (point 2), and also they might well recognise that rules and regulations bind managers as well as employees (point 4). So bureaucracy in this sense it can be found to some extent in the private sector, especially regarding dimensions 2, 4 and 7. "Bureaucracy" does not mean "a public system".

The pure form is never met in reality. For one thing, members of organisations continually hide behind the rules while favouring their own interests; the condition that they should operate in the organisation's interests is normally only partially met. For another, the ideal form falls short when rapid changes of the organisational tasks are required. But the purity of the design serves to reveal the nature of the bureaucratic reality through departure from the ideal form – imprecise rules often not observed, areas of autonomy built up in order to resist control procedures, external supports to balance internal pressures. Alternative organisational forms are responses to the limitations of bureaucracies, such as lack of adaptability and the stifling of individual initiatives and spontaneity but they do not usually fundamentally challenge the important dimensions of bureaucracy to do with hierarchy, standardisation and control.

The strength of the scenario approach lies in establishing distance between an intellectual fiction and complex realities as a means to acquire a better understanding of commonalities and differences between "real" organisations (firms, schools, hospitals, churches, and non-profit organisations) and an intellectual design. As regards bureaucracy, this methodology provides useful insights on the different forms it may take and the degree to which it is present. The OECD "Schooling for Tomorrow" scenarios can be understood as a kind of *ideal-type methodology* which seeks to describe in words what could happen to the education system under different proposals on specific dimensions – using the *if …then* rationale. The scenarios are social constructions devised by individuals able to design from scratch several models built on the same dimensions. They are the product of an *ex post* rationalisation and their fruitfulness lies in their capacity to provoke.

Different questions can be asked of the scenarios. They may be a tool to discuss which futures are preferred or disliked, or are likely or unlikely (Hutmacher, 2001). Such a tool may help to pin down the direction of observable trends towards or away from the different scenarios (as dealt with in workshops in the Poitiers 2003 OECD "Schooling for Tomorrow" Forum). However, answers to such questions as "how near to or far away from each scenario is your school system?" or "with which scenario are current educational policies in your system most and least consistent?" depend on the status of those within the education structure giving the answers. Any particular perception is a point of view which comes from a particular location in the structure: the views of teaching staff, for example, are not the same as those of the managers. Hence, the varying perception of possible future evolutions may well mean that this use of scenarios is more revealing of *patterns* of viewpoints than of a *general* consensus regarding the future. The variety of meaning comes also from the experience, as well as the situation, of those being asked to react to the different models. Piaget long ago labelled this approach *constructivist*. "School" as a word only makes sense through experience and acquires a value because it is collectively shared, rather than in a more objective sense. Different stakeholders develop different, perhaps conflicting, interpretations filtered through their experiences of schooling, and their own values as former students or as parents observing their children.

The richness of the scenario approach is in its capacity to reveal changing situations and to make explicit hidden variables or implicit assumptions. Take the OECD's "re-schooling" scenarios. They embody an implicit view of organisational forms which builds on the sociological thesis about emerging new mechanisms for co-ordinating and controlling different sectors of the economy. According to this thesis, organisational structures that are large and centralised and have relied on control and communications channels are vanishing because they are ineffective. Such vertically-integrated structures are implicitly the "bureaucratic scenario", another of the OECD set. In line with the thesis, they are dinosaurs: ill-adapted to a changing environment and a growing variety of unstable demands, including those of a knowledge-based economy.

Evidence is lacking with which to evaluate the performance of the emergent new forms of organisation underpinning "re-schooling". The existence of routines should not be confused with "red tape" – organisational theories have shown that routines can actually generate innovations. One needs to distinguish two types of innovation: one devoted to exploring new frontiers, the other about continuous efforts for doing, exploiting or renewing existing procedures. Within an organisation, these two dimensions of exploration and exploitation are not given equal weight, with exploitation typically more important than exploration.

## The methodological challenge of international comparisons

There are also methodological difficulties with establishing fruitful international comparisons of the scenarios. Even if comparisons are widely developed by international organisations (such as through the PISA surveys of student achievement), they actually make demanding theoretical and methodological assumptions giving rise to challenging questions. What is the specific objective, explicit and implicit, of the international comparison? How to deal with the societal dimension? Can there be a "culture-free" approach?

Different approaches to international comparisons are:

- As *societal facts considered as universals* which can be identified. This approach is implicit in building indicators such as of reading literacy or mathematics achievement levels. These indicators are useful for comparing different types of countries but dramatically reduce complexity. Even such a standard indicator as level of female employment covers a very wide range of factors: in order to compare country A with B, it is important to know what are the access tracks for women to enter the labour market, types of existing services for child-care, the extent of family involvement and support for salaried mothers, tax arrangements in relation to child-care costs, and so forth.

- The second approach is a *cultural or anthropological* one, and consists of identifying *unique characteristics* with which to specify a society taken as a whole. This approach focuses on unique features which "sum up" a mode of social relations, such as hierarchy versus contractualisation. This approach facilitates comparison and avoids misleading interpretations of indicators. For example, using indicators to compare cultural policies in France and the United States, it is necessary to take account of private foundations enjoying tax expenditures for the United States while public funding is dominant in France.

- The third approach can be labelled as *"institutional"*, and focuses on *the national institutions embedded in historical tracks*. OECD has analysed national systems of innovation, for instance, and this approach reveals a path dependency specific to each country in analysing public innovation policies. Turning from innovation to education, national institutions have their own definition regarding "education" or "schooling" – each country develops its own answer and invents its proper organisational tool for achieving common goals.

What are the consequences of this variety of approaches for the scenario methodology? The first approach is implicitly "culture-free" and implies an underlying common set of relationships but with the education system itself considered as a "black box". This conception allows the performance of one system to be compared with another one with the challenge being to identify appropriate indicators for this purpose. Differential performance may be *explained* by pointing to cultural traits (which are at the heart of the second approach). Once the "black box" is opened, however, the anthropological dimension comes to the fore meaning that a public activity like education has then to be understood in terms of values and norms. The institutional approach allows for "equi-finality" – that two countries might obtain the same results using different organisational models – and avoids the assumption that there is "one-best" way.

## The normative and socio-technical dimensions

A challenge facing the OECD "Schooling for Tomorrow" project using scenarios is to match the *map* and the *territory*. The map is a transcript. To design a scenario is to act as a map-maker where each scenario is a map in itself which builds up an image of what an education system might be in the future. A map is clearly different from the territory it portrays, just as at a restaurant the menu (transcript) is not the same as the food we are served. One strength of the scenario methodology is that it can initiate a process of feedback from the users of "maps" to the "map-makers" who designed them whereby the user can help identify inconsistencies and inaccuracies.

A common way to map possible trajectories is through using the spaces defined by two cross-cutting dimensions. Below I outline what I think are key dimensions, before combining them to create scenarios. One deals with normative contents and expectations about schooling and can be labelled the *"value line"*; consistent with the map metaphor we can say it runs north/south. The other "east-west" dimension is the socio-technical aspect of schooling – the *"supply line"* – which is the delivery function for a school considered as a system.

### The value line – the "social to individual" authority dimension

This line seeks to capture the range of values within which schooling is evolving. The north pole is the strong *societal orientation* and at the south is the strong *individualistic orientation*. In reality, schools are embedded within a society somewhere between the extreme poles. To the north, education is socially oriented and schools are aimed at cohesion, equity and reproduction. The south side is individualistically oriented, and schooling increasingly geared to its clients as consumers. These two poles express a range of values of how people are bound together in social arrangements in which schools are an integral part. This dimension is essentially about authority and its impact on values (Figure 3.1).

**Figure 3.1. From north to south – societal to individualistic orientations towards schooling**

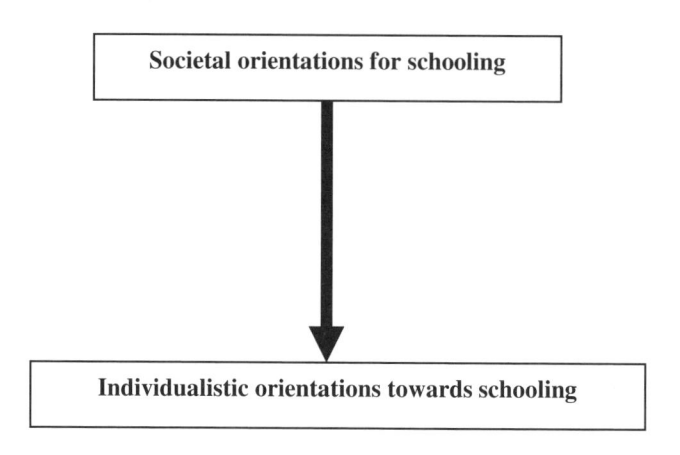

```
┌─────────────────────────────────────┐
│  Societal orientations for schooling │
└─────────────────────────────────────┘
                  │
                  ▼
┌─────────────────────────────────────────┐
│ Individualistic orientations towards schooling │
└─────────────────────────────────────────┘
```

*Source*: Author.

What is specific to the teaching function is the management of authority, which sociologists refers to as the "transmission function" of education – how people come to the values and norms which define society, citizenship, and behaviour. Schools produce images of the world as do families and the other strategic institutions which produce and reproduce society. The teacher is transmitting a public image of humanity, of space (geography) and time (history). As Norbert Elias (1998) puts it:

*Under the cover of what adults think and plan, the relationship that forms between them and the young has functions and effects in the latter's personalities which they do not intend and of which they scarcely know.*

This can be characterised as an "institutional programme" – with a strong state and stable institutions which produce a framework of social statuses well understood by individuals. The teacher is an active part of this process and the school a key part of the social fabric. Values are internalised within this specific space – and in a limited time period, crucial if children and youngsters are to be moulded before they reach adulthood.

Moving beyond the dimension itself to look at on-going trends, one can observe a weakening of the authority dimension of schooling. This is manifest in the decline of the institutional programme *i.e.* a movement away from the north end of the values dimension, though the decline is happening in different ways and at different speeds among OECD countries. The daily reproduction of social norms and symbolic signals is more and more under the scrutiny of interest groups advocating the right to deliver their own values for their children. Religious groups are an obvious source of the change but also certain ethnic communities or even just disappointed parents who want to educate their own children with their own values. These groups challenge the monopoly and legitimacy of schools to distil social values, as they do the objectivity of schools and the scientific approach of teachers.

The general trend is towards the disappearance of consensus about schooling in parallel with declining belief in marriage as an institution or the norms surrounding seniority: it is the individual who is in charge of his/her own life without referring to social norms diffused through institutions. The institutions meanwhile are slowly melting down. Schools are working out how to evolve in the cultural era of rational choice *i.e.* the southern pole of the value line. Individuals are making decisions and acquiring knowledge through different networks, through newspapers or the television, or the Web. Opinions are formed through informal discussion with parents and friends rather than recourse to an external scientific authority: "my opinion is as worthwhile as the teacher's".

This trend helps to explain why the idea of national education as an institution is less and less understood, not only by parents but by students, who assess themselves through their own subjectivity and their own ways of thinking and feeling. The consequence of this move down the values dimension is to reduce teaching to a matter of competence only, not competence *and* authority. The teacher is then simply the provider of services, and parents expect from the school a service delivery to fulfil their child's needs which – by definition and in their own eyes – are very specific. Each child has a potential to be discovered by the teacher. For parents, it is the future of their offspring that matters and whether this is met privately or publicly is not a major concern so long as their ends are achieved. The relationship between ends and means is weak and the best structure is one which deals most effectively with the needs of the student. If the private sector performs better, it will be chosen on grounds of its performance. The more that societies move south along the axis, the more the struggle between the private and public sectors is over.

## The supply line – from closed to open systems

A system is a recognisable entity into which different types of resources are the inputs and out of which come products or services. This is represented on this axis which can be labelled as the "supply line". The west pole defines services delivered within *closed system thinking*; the east pole is producing services within *open system thinking* on a much more piecemeal basis (Figure 3.2).

**Figure 3.2. From west to east – closed to open systems of delivery**

```
┌──────────────┐                              ┌──────────────┐
│ Closed system│ ───────────────────────────▶ │ Open system  │
└──────────────┘                              └──────────────┘
```

*Source*: Author.

Schools considered as *closed systems* means they are sufficiently independent as to allow most of their services to be analysed by reference to internal structures, ways and means: *e.g.* time management of teachers aimed at the optimisation of their presence on the site, the allocation of scarce budgetary resources for additional activities, or the application of standard operating pedagogical procedures. The "core competence" for teaching is certified through a university degree, the pedagogical techniques are taught, and trainee teachers prepared by trainers or on the job. A teacher is not just a capacity to transmit codified knowledge efficiently and indeed it is common to refer to the "art of teaching". Different kinds of knowledge are needed to make teaching effective: knowledge why, knowledge what, knowledge how. The "knowledge how" to teach is the most difficult to acquire and defines a "good teacher" for the parents and students. Hargreaves (2000) uses the expression "tinkering" to illuminate this aspect of the job. Students are not ignored in the closed system but they are internal factors within it, managed in terms of *flows* from grade to grade. The assessment procedures are available for all without distinction. Schools distribute rewards and punishments through specific rules and internal committees. Tight integration, co-ordination, and control aim to ensure stability, which become ends in themselves rather than means to an end. There is concentration on the principles of internal organisational functioning.

Schools in an *open system* recognise the "equi-finality" principle – that there are more ways than one of producing a given outcome. Teaching remains an art but the open system needs considerably more organisation and management in the classroom. Why? Because the variety of demands has to be matched by a variety of the supply of education through different pedagogical exercises, workshops, lectures, timing, etc. The autonomy of schools in an open system allows initiatives coming from both the inside and the outside without the constraints of controls from a central authority. Schools are open from early in the morning to late at night to allow for continuing education, with classrooms redesigned for these purposes. Continuous feedback is at work *i.e.* schools adjust for their own malfunctioning and cope with changes in their environments. In terms of services provided, schools offer a piece-meal service around a compulsory core of courses. Options or electives do not come from the supply side (*i.e.* the teachers who propose to open electives in the discipline they are familiar with) but from a consensus of all the stakeholders.

## The four quadrants as scenarios

If these two lines are crossed – the "values" line and the "supply" line – the quadrants of these dimensions combined give four new scenarios, which can be used to understand the path dependency which makes schools move from one quadrant to another and the implications of so doing (Figure 3.3).

The NW quadrant can be labelled the *conservation scenario*, corresponding to the "Status quo" of the OECD scenario set. To conserve a position does not necessarily mean to stand still as there is asymmetry between changing and not changing. Political forces or policies advocating change need to justify these to those who resist, such as strongly-unionised teachers. Why change? What are the new goals? Change for what, for whom? A variety of self-defensive mechanisms may come into play in this quadrant in order to ensure either no change or that the change which takes place is only cosmetic.

The SW scenario can be labelled the *survival scenario*. Institutions always seek survival and so they will accept some change if threatened so long as it does not damage internal structures. Typically, it might be seen in the reinforcement of coaching for specific students unable to follow the rest of the class or the increased use of ICT to allow each student to progress at its own speed – teachers are giving up some of their authority and new personnel are being brought into the educational function. Teacher's unions become more focused on fringes and benefits and not stuck in ideological positions. The rhetoric about the educational function of schooling declines compared with that regarding the linkage between school and employment.

The NE quadrant can be labelled the *transformation scenario*. The authority function of teaching is maintained through the recruitment of new teachers eager to maintain this function while the school is receptive to outside influences as it is an open system. The result is a change to a more complex structure. Schools learn how to map their environment and how to select and shape their organisational and managerial responses such as through creating new services, involving parents in the decision-making process, and strengthening leadership and the autonomy of the school as a unit.

The SE quadrant can be labelled as the *market scenario*. The competence function dominates over the authority function through the recruitment of new teachers who focus on pedagogical techniques and student results on whose support they depend. Schools manage private funds from fees and public funds from vouchers. Parents and local authorities are key actors in managing the schools, recruiting teachers through *ad hoc* committees. Private companies sponsor the education market and supply textbooks and pedagogical materials.

**Figure 3.3. The four scenarios of the quadrant analysis**

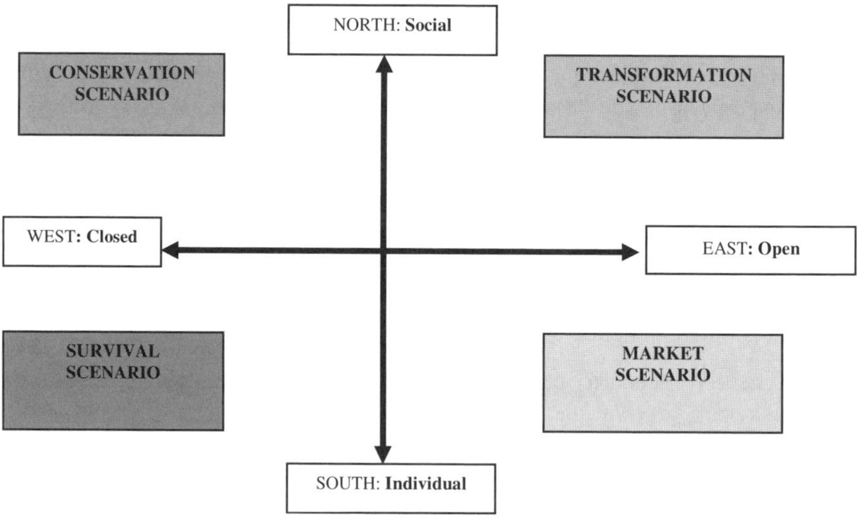

*Source*: Author.

# Moving around the quadrants – what makes for change from one scenario to another

Each of the quadrants or new scenarios represents a stable position in terms of these two key dimensions. Movement between them indicates strategic change and it can then be asked: what are the social forces which stimulate such moves?

## *Shifting down the values axis*

If an outside pressure – from politicians, parents, international benchmarks, scarcity of resources, and so forth – successfully breaks into the closed system it is a form of *"environmental intrusion"* making possible a move from the NW (conservation) to the SW (survival) quadrant. Such a pressure to bring about a survival response might be, for instance, new requirements for students to pass or succeed within shorter time horizons. Another example could be coaching at home increasing the pressure of private competition on the public system from parents expecting good marks for their children. Attrition of human resources may also be a signal for change. The technocracy would not want to lose its pre-eminent position in setting rules and procedures for the periphery, and would bow to pressure if it felt this position was threatened. Teachers unions may also support the move in this direction if they judge that it will be less threatening than the conceivable alternatives, and so might fall in line in order to keep basic structures, contracts and privileges in place.

Another move down the axis, this time from NE (transformation) to SE (market) may be triggered by stakeholders eager to transform radically the organisation and management of schools. Such stakeholders as local politicians, parents, or firms may not agree to a compromise in which school becomes an open system but not within terms and values they share. They believe that change has not gone far enough, and may perceive the resistance to come mainly from the educational workforce. To move down this part of the value line thus supposes weak teachers unions unable to resist to the pressures exerted and isolated from public opinion and the media. As the move takes place, schools turn out into networks of contracts, outsourcing maintenance, control activities, and teaching. Teachers are recruited on a short-term basis and periodically evaluated by their peers and parents.

## Shifting along the supply axis

The move from west to east is quite conceivable today through the public pressure of opinion which does not believe that in a changing environment schools should be in a closed system. The situation might well be different were the system efficient but international benchmark surveys such as PISA show that performance is not well correlated with mechanistic structures consuming heavy financial resources. There is not an organisational optimum for producing results.

This move can be triggered by politicians eager to radically overhaul the administrative structure without changing the recruitment process of teachers, who are mainly civil servants. Why such a move? It may come from the allocation dilemma between tertiary and secondary education. It may be agreed that public money must be spent as a priority on the tertiary sector for competitiveness reasons, leading to the pursuit of alternatives for the schools. It could also be due to the pressure coming from young, demanding parents. The move along this axis can be seen as a re-engineering of the central administrative procedures through massive decentralisation. Decision-making processes are re-designed and the school comes up more and more as an autonomous unit of management headed by professional managers. A trade-off may be negotiated between the unions and the policy makers – increased variety and a new type of organisation vs. stability in the recruitment through meritocratic competition and seniority rules. The direct move from the SW quadrant (survival) to the SE (market) seems improbable because it would be such a wrench; the pathway instead might be SW to NE (transformation) and then possibly to the SE once the system has been opened up.

This map or quadrant tool facilitates the understanding of the dynamics of transformation of the school system by moving around the quadrants horizontally and vertically. Transversal moves indicate the scope of change of the throughput – different modes of co-ordination, recruitment of teachers with different profiles, teachers vs. coaches – while the values about national education are maintained. Vertical moves indicate the transformation and reorganisation of the public image of the schooling system, which is changing through the pressure coming from different "external" stakeholders such as parents, service providers, mass media, and employers.

# *References*

Elias, N. (1998), *On Civilisation, Power, and Knowledge: Selected Writings*, edited by Stephen Mennell and Johan Goudsblom, University of Chicago Press, Chicago.

Hargreaves (2000), "The Production Mediation and Use of Professional Knowledge among Teachers and Doctors: A Comparative Analysis", *Knowledge Management in the Learning Society,* OECD, Paris.

Hutmacher, W. (2001), "Visions of Decision-makers and Educators for the Future of Schools", *What Schools for the Future?,* Chapter 12, OECD, Paris.

Weber, M. (1904), "Objectivity", *Archiv fur Socialwissenschaft un Socialpolitik,* reprinted in various sociological readers.

Weber, M. (1946), *Essays in Sociology*, Oxford University Press, New York, pp. 196-204.

Weber, M. (1947), *The Theory of Social and Economic Organisation*, The Free Press, Glencoe, Ill., pp. 329-336.

# Chapter 4
# Scenario development: a typology of approaches

by
Philip van Notten[1]

*On the basis of a definition that draws on a wide understanding of the field, Philip van Notten proposes and discusses a typology of scenario methods. This is divided into three "macro" characteristics – goals, design and content – and ten "micro" characteristics within these broad categories. This typology demonstrates the diversity of scenario approaches and the ways and contexts in which they are used, as well as the output they produce. The chapter looks at the organisational cultures and arrangements which can help make scenario exercises most effective, and closes with observations about the value of very long-term thinking.*

## What is a scenario?

*"The real voyage of discovery consists not in seeking new landscapes but in having new eyes."*

Marcel Proust

The word "scenario" is derived from the Latin *scaena*, meaning scene (Ringland, 1998). The term was originally used in the context of such performing arts as theatre and film. Kahn (Ringland, 1998) adopted the term

---

[1] The author is a researcher and consultant in the area of scenario analysis and foresight. The chapter draws on his dissertation, Van Notten (2005).

because of its emphasis on storytelling but the use of the term varies. Sparrow (2000) notes four contemporary uses of the word.

- One use corresponds to *sensitivity analysis*, whether in cash flow management, risk assessment, or project management.

- A second, as used in military or civil emergency planning, is synonymous with the idea of a *contingency plan* defining who is to do what during a particular event.

- A third sense is also synonymous with a *contingency plan* but applied to decision-making in *corporate or public policy*.

- Sparrow argues that planners advising decision makers use a fourth interpretation, regarding scenarios as more *exploratory* so that a scenario is less a strategy and more a *coherently structured speculation*. While the distinction is not always recognised (*e.g.* Godet and Roubelat, 1996), this fourth meaning forms the basis for much of the interest of scenarios for education.

There are thus varying definitions of "scenario" but on one point there is consensus: *it is not a prediction* (Van der Heijden *et al.*, 2002). Characteristics inherent in the various definitions include that they are: hypothetical, causally coherent, internally consistent, and/or descriptive. A definition which covers many of the characteristics proposed by others is:

*Scenarios are consistent and coherent descriptions of alternative hypothetical futures that reflect different perspectives on past, present, and future developments, which can serve as a basis for action. (Van Notten, 2005)*

Scenario development emerged following World War II in US military strategic planning with the RAND Corporation, and in French spatial planning at DATAR. In the 1960s, General Electric and Royal Dutch Shell introduced scenario techniques in their corporate planning procedures and in the 1970s scenarios achieved prominence in speculations about the future of society, the economy and the environment. The 1972 Club of Rome report *The Limits to Growth* is one of the most famous and controversial examples of such a study. Today, scenarios are used in a wide range of contexts: by small and medium-sized enterprises (SMEs), to regional and national foresight studies, to environmental assessments for public policy such as the UN' Environmental Programme *Global Environmental Outlook* or the RIVM Netherlands Institute of Public Health and the Environment.

The variety of contemporary scenario practice is suggested by the wide range of bodies using them, including multinationals, government departments at various levels, and temporary bodies such as national foresight programmes. A limited number of private organisations like Shell and DaimlerChrysler have institutionalised the use of scenarios. They are developed and applied on an ad hoc basis, however, by many organisations including those oriented to short-term market change, such as the telecom companies KPN, Ericsson, and Vodafone. Scenario development is not common in SMEs, although two documented examples are the mail-order company Smith & Hawken (Schwartz, 1991) and Flight Directors, a broker company between airlines and holiday companies (Fuller et al., 2003). Another form of scenario work developed in the past 15 years has been through inter-company co-operation, facilitated by organisations such as GBN and the World Business Council for Sustainable Development (WBCSD).

## A typology of scenario characteristics

There are several scenario typologies available, such as those proposed by Ducot and Lubben (1980), Duncan and Wack (1994), Godet and Roubelat (1996), Postma *et al.* (1995), and Heugens and Van Oosterhout (2001). Each of these identifies fundamental distinctions between scenario types, but as the typologies reflect the state of play at the time, they become outdated as the field evolves. Another problem is that typologies often fail to capture the full range of contemporary scenario development. Heugens and Van Oosterhout's typology is more recent than Ducot and Lubben's but less detailed. Business-oriented classifications such as Duncan and Wack's do not take account of differences between macro-economic and environmental scenarios. Therefore, the existing classifications are a source of inspiration but not detailed enough for an in-depth analysis, nor broad enough to do justice to the variety of today's scenario development approaches.

Given the different limitations, I developed a new typology on the basis of earlier typologies and a comparative review of approximately 100 studies carried out since the mid-1980s. These studies were conducted in different organisational settings, including businesses such as the British Airways and KPMG; "inter-company" co-operative efforts such as the Dutch Management Association (NIVE) and the World Business Council for Sustainable Development (WBCSD); governmental organisations such as the Rotterdam Port Authority; broadly-based participatory futures initiatives such as those carried out in South Africa and Colombia; and academic studies such as the Intergovernmental Panel on Climate Change (IPCC) and the research institutes of the VISIONS project. The studies reviewed covered either a range of sectors (transport, telecom, and nutrition), or national and regional development strategies; or were defined by issues such as gender equality, the labour market, climate change, and leadership.

The typology (Table 4.1) identifies three broad "macro" characteristics which are central aspects of scenarios and their development. The macro characteristics apply both to sets of scenarios and to individual scenarios. They address the "why?" "how?" and "what?" of a scenario study: its goals, the design of the process, and the scenario contents. The project's goals influence the design influencing in turn contents.

A rudimentary comparison of scenario analyses might confine itself to the use of the macro characteristics. A more in-depth comparison demands a greater appreciation of detail, which can be gained with the help of nine micro characteristics that are described in the following paragraphs. They are categorised according to the macro characteristic to which they are closest associated.

### Table 4.1. A typology of scenario characteristics

| Broad "macro" characteristics | Detailed "micro" characteristics |
|---|---|
| The goals of scenario studies<br>Exploration – Pre-policy research | The function of the scenario exercise<br>Process – Product |
| | The role of values in the scenario process<br>Descriptive – Normative |
| | The subject area covered<br>Issue-based – Area based – Institutional based |
| | The nature of change addressed<br>Evolutionary – Discontinuity (Abrupt – Gradual discontinuity) |
| Design of the scenario process<br>Intuitive – Analytical | Inputs into the scenario process<br>Qualitative – Quantitative |
| | Methods employed in the scenario process<br>Participatory – Model-based |
| | Groups involved in the scenario process<br>Inclusive – Exclusive |
| Content of the scenarios<br>Complex – Simple | The role of time in the scenario<br>Chain – Snapshot |
| | Issues covered by the scenario<br>Heterogeneous – Homogeneous |
| | Level of integration<br>Integration – Fragmented |

*Source*: Author.

The comparison of scenario analyses can confine itself to the broad macro features. In-depth comparison demands a greater appreciation of detail, for which further micro characteristics are described for each.

## *The goals of scenario studies*

The educational function of scenarios has gained in importance in recent years compared with its function as a planning tool (Ringland, 1998). Scenarios began to be used more for exploratory ends than prediction, as illustrated by Royal Dutch Shell's 1972 scenarios, which raised the possibility of a transformation in the supply chain for oil production. Some leading practitioners (*e.g* Global Business Network [GBN], see Chapter 1) abandoned the planning aspect altogether, choosing instead to use scenarios primarily for learning and communication. Policy planning is still a feature of some approaches such as the French "prospective", which combines the exploratory with the decision-oriented. Even so, the decision orientation has tended to broaden and to resemble pre-policy research rather than classical planning. Scenario planners in general do not start with a narrow focus, doing so increases the chances of missing key determinants of future conditions or events (Duncan and Wack, 1994).

There are thus two poles of the spectrum in relation to goals – exploration and pre-policy research. *Exploration* covers learning, awareness-raising, the stimulation of creative thinking, and investigating the interaction of societal processes (Schwartz, 1991; European Environment Agency and ICIS, 2000; Van der Heijden, 1996). In exploratory scenario exercises, the process may well be as important as the product. The "Which World?: Scenarios for the 21$^{st}$ Century" (Hammond, 1998) is a good example of an exploratory exercise investigating possible paths to alternative futures. In *pre-policy research*, on the other hand, scenarios are used to examine paths to futures that vary according to their desirability. Decision support scenarios may be variously described as desirable, optimistic, high-road, or utopic; conventional or middle-of-the-road; and undesirable, pessimistic, low-road, dystopic, or doom scenarios. High- and low-road scenarios were developed in the Scenarios for Scotland study (McKiernan *et al.*, 2001a, b, c), and they are implied in the Mont Fleur (Kahane, 1998) and the Destino Colombia scenarios (Global Business Network, 1998). Pre-policy research scenarios may propose concrete options for strategic decision-making, such as those reported in Gertner and Knez (2000) and Van Notten (2000). It is more common in pre-policy research scenario exercises to offer implicit policy recommendations. The most desirable Mont Fleur scenario, for example – the Flight of the Flamingos –

describes a South Africa successfully negotiating the post-apartheid transition period, but does so only in general policy terms.

In practice, studies are often hybrids straddling the two poles of exploration and pro policy research (Van der Heijden, 1996). In a first phase, scenarios may be developed in exploration of a field which will often be too general to serve as the basis for decision-making. Therefore, new scenarios may then be developed using the exploration of the first phase to zoom in on aspects relevant to strategy development. For example, at Royal Dutch Shell, global scenarios are developed on a corporate level which are then used to help develop the second set of scenarios focused on the strategic issues most relevant to individual Shell operating companies (*ibid.*).

*The function of the scenario exercise*

*Process-oriented* scenario development functions to promote: learning, communication, and improving observational skills. The learning/educative function is about informing people (Van der Heijden *et al.*, 2002) by deciphering the often confusing overload of information (Duncan and Wack, 1994), and integrating possible future events and developments into consistent pictures of the future. Making sense of the future in this way can challenge mental models and prevailing mind-sets (Wack, 1985; Schoemaker, 1995), and can involve learning from the past and investigating fundamental uncertainties about the future. The educational aspect of scenario development may well serve to improve participants' intellectual and creative skills (Van der Heijden, 1996). Ultimately, scenarios might serve as a vehicle to instil a consciousness of the future in society (Van Steenbergen, 2003). Scenarios may also have a communicative function (Van der Heijden *et al.*, 2002; Masini and Vasquez, 2000). The process of scenario development provides a language to cross disciplinary boundaries. In organisations, it may provide a basis for "strategic conversations", to discuss perceptions on strategy, opportunities, and threats. Social interaction in a scenario process arguably helps an organisation to improve its perceptive ability to anticipate both difficult times and upcoming opportunities (Schwartz, 1991).

*Product-oriented* scenario studies are more concerned with the nature and quality of the output than with how it was arrived at. Their functions are: the identification of driving forces and signs of emerging trends, policy development, and to test policy. Scenarios can be used to identify and prioritise the dangers and opportunities in emerging events and processes (Masini and Vasquez, 2000), signs of which are sometimes referred to as "weak signals", "early warnings", "seeds" or "traces". Scenarios may also be a tool for evaluating decisions and testing policy options by doing "practice runs" of possible future situations which indicate the possible effects of decisions (Van der Heijden *et al.*, 2002; Wilson, 2000).

*The role of values in the scenario process*

Some might say that all scenarios are normative in that they reflect interpretations, values, and the interests of those involved in the scenario exercise. It is nevertheless useful to distinguish between *descriptive* scenarios and those which are explicitly *normative*. Royal Dutch Shell's 2001 global scenarios entitled Business Class and Prism, for example, outline two possible futures without indications of desirability (Shell International, 2002). In contrast we can refer to the "Balanced Growth" scenario in The Netherlands in Triplicate study (CPB Netherlands Bureau for Economic Policy Analysis, 1992), as normative because the explicit aim is to show, given certain conditions, that economic growth can go hand in hand with environmental protection.

Whether a scenario looks forwards from the present situation to the future or back to the present from a particular future end point can have a bearing on whether it is normative or not. For instance, the backward-looking "back-casting" scenario (Robinson, 1990) is explicitly normative in its analysis of the measures and developments needed to reach a particular point in the future judged to be desirable. An example of back-casting is the POSSUM project (Banister *et al.*, 2000) which formulated sustainable transport targets for the year 2020. However, not all backward-looking scenarios are explicitly normative as the descriptions in the literature on anticipatory scenarios demonstrate (Ducot and Lubben, 1980).

*The subject area covered*

The subject covered provides the focus to scenarios. The time scale adopted is one way in which focus is determined, though the perception of time is dependent on context. Ten years is considered as the long term in the fashion industry whereas it is relatively short term for many environmental issues. Broadly 25 years or more may be considered long term scale for a scenario exercise as with the World Business Council for Sustainable Development's (WBCSD) global scenarios until the year 2050 (1998). A time scale of 3 to 10 years may be thought of as short term for scenario work, illustrated by the study of the food and beverage market by a Dutch nutrition company (Van Notten, 2000). Due to its dependency on context, time is not here proposed as a characteristic of the typology in its own right.

Yet, time scale is certainly relevant for establishing focus with regards to the *issue,* the geographical *area* and the *institution* the scenarios address.

Issue-based scenarios take societal questions as the subject of study, such as the future of television (Digital Thinking Network, 2000), or the future of women (McCorduck and Ramsey, 1996). Area-based scenarios explore futures for a particular continental region, country, region or city. There are also examples which address the global scale – the OECD scenarios in the world in 2020 (OECD, 1997) and the IPCC scenarios (Intergovernmental Panel on Climate Change, 2000). There is also a large number of examples addressing the national level such as Japan (Nakamae, 1998), Destino Colombia (Global Business Network, 1998), and the Netherlands in 2030 study, which developed spatial planning futures. An example of regional scenarios is provided by a case study that is part of the Netherlands in 2030 study on scenarios for agriculture and land-use in the Dutch province of Noord Brabant (Stuurgroep Toekomstonderzoek en Strategisch Omgevingsbeleid, 2000).

Institution-based scenarios address the spheres of interest of an organisation, group of organisations, or sector. They can be broadly subdivided into macro or contextual scenarios, on the one hand, and focused or transactional scenarios, on the other (Van der Heijden, 1996). (Related terms for macro scenarios are "global", "archetypal", "framework" and "external"; for meso scenarios, they are "decision" and "internal".) The "contextual scenario" is about the institution's environment and the issues that they do not directly influence themselves. Contextual analyses can explore unfamiliar terrain as was the case in Shell's global scenarios. A "transactional scenario" refers to the institution's meso-environment and focuses on the interactions between variables and dynamics within a particular field. However, the distinction between the contextual and transactional environments may not always be clearcut. The different institution-based spheres are shown in Figure 4.1.

A study can combine scenarios based on issues, areas, and institutions to create systemic scenarios cutting across all these dimensions. For example, the VISIONS scenarios (Rotmans *et al.*, 2000) are both area- and issue-based in their exploration of equity, employment, and consumption in a European context; the drinks company United Distillers' scenarios of India and South Africa are both institution- and area-based (Ringland, 1998).

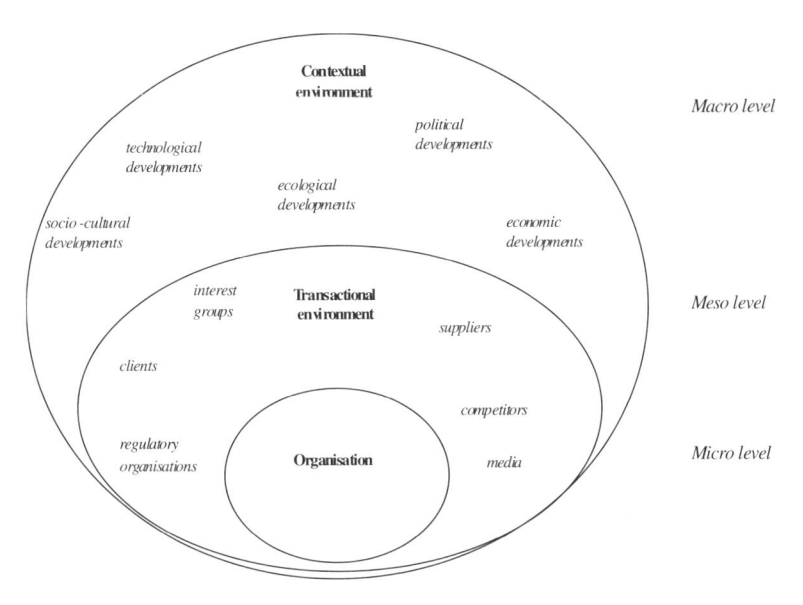

**Figure 4.1. The levels and focus of institution-based scenarios**

```
                    Contextual
                    environment
                                      political          Macro level
       technological              developments
       developments
                            ecological
                            developments
   socio-cultural                            economic
   developments                              developments

              interest    Transactional                   Meso level
              groups      environment
                                        suppliers
           clients

                                        competitors
       regulatory                                         Micro level
       organisations   Organisation
                                        media
```

*Source*: Author.

## The nature of change addressed

In the *nature of change* addressed in the scenarios, one can distinguish between evolutionary developments and discontinuities. Evolutionary scenarios are consistent with the notion of a gradual, incremental unfolding of a world pattern or system through time and space; Brooks (1986) and Morgan (2002) argue that this is the dominant scenario paradigm within which it is difficult, if not impossible, even to imagine discontinuity, let alone incorporate it into scenarios. The 1996 British Airways study (Moyer, 1996) is a noteworthy illustration of one which assumed that the future would not significantly vary from the past. Airline regulation changes and IT developments are considered, but judged to be driving forces powerful enough to cause a significant deviation of current trends.

The sudden nature of change is the distinguishing feature of abrupt discontinuities. They give society a jolt, though possibly only a temporary and reversible one. Abrupt discontinuity manifests itself through events but these tend to be connected to underlying processes. Gradual discontinuity, on the other hand, is a self-reinforcing process of societal transformation where a diverse set of developments – socio-cultural, technological, economic, environmental, and political – converges. The distinction between abrupt and gradual discontinuity is not always clear, however, as what constitutes a discontinuity depends on the time scale and the disciplinary perspective from which it is regarded.

The biotechnology scenarios developed by the World Business Council for Sustainable Development (2000) include examples of both forms of discontinuity. In "The Domino Effect" Scenario, biotechnology continues to make steady progress until 2010, when an abrupt discontinuity occurs following the deaths of 25 patients undergoing gene therapy which are given enormous media attention resulting in the collapse of the biotechnology business. The other two scenarios portray worlds of gradual discontinuity over a 50-year period. The "Hare and the Tortoise" Scenario describes societal transformation towards traditional farming techniques and holistic health remedies, and away from biotechnology. The Biotrust Scenario describes a transition to a world where biotechnology is a trusted and integral part of the human fabric with many applications in health care, food production, and life sciences.

## *Design of the scenario process*

The second broad macro dimension of the typology addresses the methodological aspects of scenario development. Numerous scenario communities have developed over the years, each with its own approaches. A basic distinction is between analytical and intuitive designs. On *analytical* approaches, for example, the European environmental scenario community, which includes the Stockholm Environment Institute (SEI), the Austria-based International Institute for Applied Systems Analysis (IIASA), and the Dutch National Institute of Public Health and the Environment (RIVM), often uses computer simulations. The security and defence sectors draw *inter alia* on the RAND Corporation's scenario work. The business community is drawn strongly to the Anglo-American approaches of Royal Dutch Shell and GBN, while the French "prospective" approach leans more strongly than they do on computer software. German scenario work is known for its analytical rigour, as demonstrated by DaimlerChrysler's Society and Technology Research Group and Scenario Management International (ScMI).

Model-based techniques as analytical approaches were among the earliest methods for scenario development, involving the quantification of identified uncertainties. The models used may be conceptual as well as arithmetic or computer-based. Computer simulations are more rigorous and less flexible than the intuitive approaches reviewed next. For instance, it is difficult to repeat certain steps taken in "prospectives"; relevant causal relationships often cannot be addressed in the model-based designs. Computer simulation models applied in contemporary scenario work include TARGETS and Threshold 21, which perform integrated assessments of sustainability, and WORLDSCAN, a macro-economic model applied to economic, energy, transport, trade, and environmental policy. (These are acronyms for Tool to Assess Regional and Global Environmental and Health Targets for Sustainability and WORLD model for SCenario ANalysis.)

Another analytical approach to building scenarios is desk research, developing them through document analysis or archival research. This is less formalised and systematic than the model-based forms but may be just as rigorous. Examples of scenario studies based on desk research include Bobbitt's *The Shield of Achilles* (2002), Schwartz *et al.*'s "The Long Boom" (1999), and McRae's global scenario for 2020 (1995). But desk research is not confined to any one method or scientific tradition, and covers the range from pursuit of hunches through research to the more structured procedures of data collection and analysis.

Compared with the analytical designs are the *intuitive* approaches. These importantly depend on qualitative knowledge and insights as sources from which scenarios are developed. Creative techniques such as the development of stories or storylines in workshops are good examples. The intuitive approach takes scenario development as an art form, as underlined by such titles as "The Art of the Long View" (Schwartz, 1991) and "The Art of Strategic Conversation" (Van der Heijden, 1996).

There are a number of basic steps in an intuitive scenario process: a) identification of subject or problem area; b) description of relevant factors; c) prioritisation and selection of relevant factors; d) the creation of scenarios. A subsequent step might be scenario evaluation as pre-policy research.

The above steps may be performed deductively or inductively (Van der Heijden, 1996). The deductive approach creates a framework early in the process with which to structure the rest of the scenario exercise. A two-dimensional matrix is a common method, as illustrated below, which is created by identifying the two factors considered the most influential for the topic of concern. Other relevant factors can then be arranged around this framework. Van't Klooster and Van Asselt (2006) distinguish between four ways of creating and using the matrix:

- The *backbone approach* starts from a particular theory about relationships between the factors being addressed in the scenarios, as compared with the others below which rely on pragmatic choice to provide structure to scenario development.

- The *foundation approach*, as mentioned above, reasons from two factors considered particularly important to the future of the issue in question, with which to structure the scenario development process and their interpretation.

  The scenarios on the future of the Dutch job market developed by KPMG Ebbinge (now called Ebbinge & company) were developed with the help of such a matrix, as illustrated in Figure 4.2 (de Jong, 1998). The dominant factors for the future were identified as economic relationships and organisation types, giving transaction- and relation-oriented economic relationships, on the one hand, and network and traditional organisations, on the other.

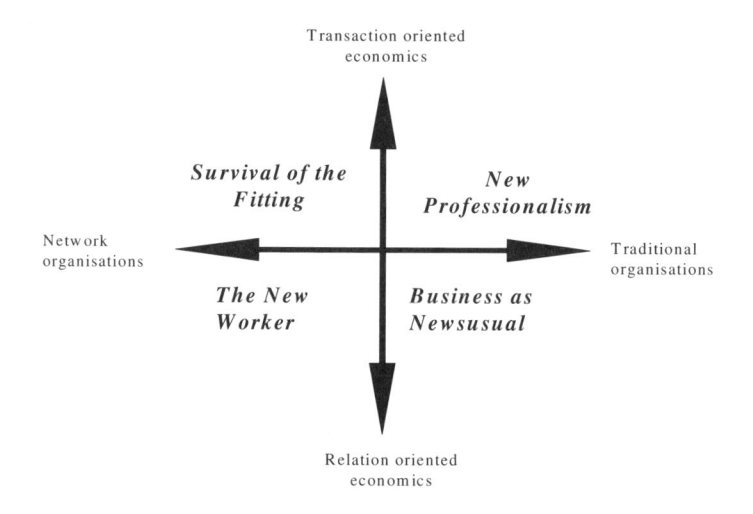

### Figure 4.2. The KPMG Ebbinge scenarios

```
                    Transaction oriented
                         economics
                             ▲
                             │
     Survival of the         │        New
        Fitting              │   Professionalism
Network                      │                    Traditional
organisations  ◄─────────────┼─────────────►      organisations
                             │
       The New               │     Business as
       Worker                │      Newsusual
                             │
                             ▼
                    Relation oriented
                        economics
```

*Source*: Author.

- By contrast, in the *scaffolding approach* the structure is abandoned as the scenarios become more elaborated.

- The *shop window approach* imposes a structure at the end of a scenario development process in order to clearly present distinctions between the scenarios.

Inductive methods, however, do not use such frameworks to impose a structure on the scenario process. Instead, they rely on a freer process, with coherent stories generated from associations, inferred causal patterns, etc. When workshops use inductive approaches, the ideas generated are often represented in a series of post-it notes arranged sequentially to form storylines. The VISIONS (Rotmans *et al.*, 2000) scenarios were developed in such a manner, although some use was made of what was called the "factor, actor, sector" framework, providing additional structure for thinking about the future.

Intuitive and analytical approaches may be used in combination. Desk research often forms part of more extensive intuitive scenario exercises, using workshops to generate creative ideas, backed up by research from the core scenario team elaborating the workshop ideas. The VISIONS project (Rotmans *et al.*, 2000) spent much time elaborating material from workshops and making it consistent and coherent. There have also been attempts to combine the two in the opposite direction. The IPCC emissions scenario (Intergovernmental Panel on Climate Change, 2000) is one where intuitive techniques support a mainly analytical approach, with narratives as a first step in the development of quantified, model-based scenarios which were then central to a global consultation with experts. However, combining intuitive approaches with model-based techniques is still experimental.

Intuitive designs are commonly used for exploratory purposes and analytical designs for pre-policy research exercises. The NIVE study (Breunesse *et al.*, 2000) on the future of leadership is an example of a purely intuitive exploratory exercise. Good examples of analytical techniques developed for pre-policy research are the Battelle Institute's BASICS and MICMAC "prospective" approach (Ringland, 1998; Godet, 1997). (The acronyms are for Battelle Scenario Inputs to Corporate Strategy and Matrice d'Impacts Croisés Multiplication Appliquée à un Classement [Cross-Impact Matrix Multiplication Applied to Classification].) Both are probabilistic computer-based models for identifying cross-impacts between variables. Further detailed distinctions to scenario processes, beyond the analytic/intuitive and deductive/inductive are provided by attention to inputs to scenario exercises, methods used, and groups involved.

*Inputs into the scenario process*

I have distinguished in the typology between *qualitative* and *quantitative* inputs used to construct and apply scenarios. Qualitative inputs are appropriate for the analysis of complex situations characterised by high levels of uncertainty, when relevant information cannot be well quantified. This might include opinions about human values and behaviour. Quantitative input is used in computer models which explore and develop energy, technology, macro-economic, and environmental forecasts.

Combining qualitative and quantitative inputs can make scenarios more consistent and robust. A quantitative scenario may be enriched and its communicability enhanced through qualitative information; a qualitative scenario may be tested for plausibility through the quantified information. Yet, the fusion of quantitative and qualitative data remains a methodological challenge.

*Methods employed in the scenario process*

The poles of development methods are *participatory* approaches, on the one hand, and *model-based* approaches, on the other. Participation is a way of collecting ideas for the scenarios such as through workshops of different stakeholders with activities adapted to the needs emerging from earlier steps in the scenario development process. Other participatory techniques include focus groups, citizens' juries and envisioning workshops. Participatory approaches are suitable for the generation of creative ideas but they will often need processing in order to enrich detail and make them coherent.

The analytical methods may use conceptual or computational models to examine possible future interactions between a selected set of variables. The computational modelling approach works mainly with quantified data, through sets of well-defined, predetermined steps. Conceptual modelling refers to the structured intellectual procedures of cross-impact and morphological analyses of "la prospective", and the techniques applied by DaimlerChrysler and ScMI. The structured approach is an especially strong feature of computational models such as the TARGETS (Rotmans and de Vries, 1997), Threshold 21 (Rorsch and de Hart, 1993) and WORLDSCAN (CPB Netherlands Bureau for Economic Policy Analysis, 1999).

Desk research is an analytical approach positioned between the participatory and the model-based methods. It usually is dependent on a single individual or small team of researchers, drawing on literature analysis or archive research. An example of such a desk study is Bobbitt's *The Shield of Achilles* (2002), which explores the history and possible futures of the "market state" based on extensive research on warfare, international relations, and international and constitutional law.

*Groups involved in the scenario process*

Group composition refers to the people involved in a scenario development process. Schoemaker (1995) among others stresses the need for management to be involved in scenario exercises if they are to have an effect on decision-making. Schwartz (1991) and Van der Heijden (1996) stress the value of "remarkable people" or imaginative individuals, whose role in scenario processes is to open the eyes of other participants to novel ideas. Civic scenarios studies such as Mont Fleur and Destino Colombia are examples where a leading principle was to have a wide cross-section of South African and Colombian society engaged in the scenario exercises.

My typology distinguishes between *inclusive* and *exclusive* groups. "Inclusive" groups bring together different types of participants in order to canvass many points of view and perspectives. The VISIONS study (Rotmans *et al.*, 2000), is a good example where the participants in the European and regional scenario development included representatives from governmental institutions, NGOs, companies, and science as well as citizens and artists from different EU member states. "Exclusive" groups have a limited variety of membership, perhaps through conscious decision. Commercial organisations, for example, mostly exclude outsiders from their scenario studies for fear of informing the competition. An outsider involved in the Telecom study (Rorsch and de Hart, 1993), for instance, had to sign a confidentiality statement.

## Content of the scenarios

The third broad macro characteristic of scenarios in the typology is their content. One can here distinguish between *complex* and *simple* scenarios. A complex scenario is composed of an intricate web of causally-related events and processes. Simple scenarios, as their name suggests, are more limited in scope; they might focus on a particular niche such as chipmaker AMD's efforts to anticipate the reactions of its competitor Intel (Gertner and Knez, 2000). Alternatively, simple scenarios may be limited to the extrapolation of a small set of isolated trends *e.g.* the European Environment Agency's baseline scenario on Europe's environment (1999). The term "simple" in this context does not imply poor quality. Indeed, scenario processes can often be criticised for excessive complexity – a simple scenario may be both more effective and less demanding of resources.

## The role of time in the scenario

Two forms of scenario can be distinguished in terms of its temporal nature: the developmental or *chain* variety on the one hand, and the end-state or *snapshot*, on the other. Chains, as in the Scenarios Europe 2010 study (Bertrand, 1999) describe the trajectory or chain of developments to a particular end-state. In this sense, they are rather like a film. Snapshot scenarios in contrast are like photos. They describe the end-state of a development path and only implicitly address the processes that resulted in that end-state. Examples of the latter are found in the NIVE scenarios on leadership in the 21$^{st}$ century (Breunesse *et al.*, 2000).

## Issues covered by the scenario

One classification of the issues covered by the scenarios distinguishes between socio-cultural, economic, and environmental factors; an institutional dimension may be included as well. Another classification is covered by the acronym STEEP which differentiates between socio-cultural, technological, economic, ecological, and political developments. The issues may refer to *heterogeneous* or *homogenous* sets of factors. UNEP's GEO-3 scenarios (2002) are scenarios which address a heterogeneous set of variables. The variables include demography, economic integration and liberalisation, social inequality, consumer culture, ICT, biotech, environmental degradation, and political decentralisation. In contrast, the KPMG scenarios (de Jong, 1998) consider only five relatively homogenous factors: employers, employees, "intermediaries", ICT, and the job market.

## Level of integration

An *integrated* scenario study is an interdisciplinary integration of relevant variables, issues and spatial scales. Examples of scenarios with a high level of cross-disciplinary synthesis are the Destino Colombia and Mont Fleur scenarios. The integration of multiple geographical scales was a key objective in VISIONS (Rotmans *et al.*, 2000) and the GEO-3 (UNEP, 2002): both scenario studies integrate global, supranational, and regional information. The alternative to the integrated approach is one where the factors are treated in relatively *isolation* one from another. An example is the sustained risk study (1994) carried out by the Netherlands Scientific Council for Government Policy (WRR). Different sectors like water, food and energy have been addressed but with little interconnection between them.

## Successful scenarios: cultures of curiosity

The typology demonstrates the diversity of contemporary scenario approaches. It also underscores the flexibility of scenario approaches in terms of the ways and contexts in which they are used, as well as the output that they produce. The flexibility in particular has its pitfalls, however, especially when, as Masini and Vasquez observe can happen, scenario development becomes "a Swiss pocket knife of multiple uses, or a magic wand"; no more than a cosmetic exercise that add a superficial legitimacy to policy-making exercises. The resulting scenarios are hollow diamonds: attractive to look at but lacking in content. One contributing factor to cosmetic scenarios is the tendency of the community of scenario practitioners to bang its own drum, where too often potential scenario pitfalls are ignored, referred to in passing or are used merely to underscore the strength to overcome them of the approach being peddled. The "what scenarios can do for you" popularisations overshadow serious discussion about pitfalls, such as those identified by Schoemaker (1998).

Another set of factors that can diminish the value of scenario exercises in practice are the stubborn effects of a particular socio-cultural or organisational environment. The "theatre" model proposed by Goffman (1959) helps to shed light on the socio-cultural dynamics that can be in play during a scenario study. The socio-cultural contexts in organisations can be divided into three areas of social reality, like the three sides of a theatre stage: front stage, backstage, and the area under the stage. The front stage is the area where the public performances are made and formal roles are played out. The backstage is the informal behind-the-scenes area of professional interaction where front stage activities are prepared and reflected on. The area under the stage is where people feel most secure and confide in one another feelings or opinions that are not expressed in the other stage areas.

"Front stage" a group may proclaim scenario work as an important tool for the facilitation of learning in organisations preparing for an uncertain future; "backstage", however, the same people implicitly, and even explicitly, may lack interest. "Front stage", uncertainty may be proclaimed as critical but in the day-to-day routines it may well not figure as an issue and career opportunism is much more important. A "front stage" official attitude may be of an uncontrollable world; "backstage", however, the "engineering attitude" prevails in the conviction that the environment can be crafted according to human needs. Publicly, a project team may be given a great deal of freedom to develop scenarios as it sees best, but "backstage" tight reins might be kept on the study. Indeed, the project team may prefer to work under the guidance of the management and the dominant mode of thinking in the organisation.

It is thus useful to look at the cultures of organisations undertaking scenario work. A precondition for any scenario development is a genuine interest in the unknowable future and challenging assumptions about it. Many scenario studies do not venture beyond the boundaries of what is known and assumed, and challenging those boundaries may even be discouraged. No matter how good a "toolbox" of methodologies and approaches might be, a scenario study is likely to fail if the interest is lacking. It is therefore inadvisable to focus on tools alone but also to invest in nurturing a "culture of curiosity".

*Cultures of curiosity* are environments driven by inquisitiveness and imaginative thinking, involving the interaction between epistemological, analytical, procedural, and contextual factors. Epistemologically, they reason from a desire to explore the future – for instance, few certainties about societal development are presumed so challenging the evolutionary paradigm that reasons from gradual, incremental change. At an analytical level, discontinuity is a source of interest rather than of discomfort – terms, metaphors and examples denoting change are common as compared with those conveying continuity. Cultures of curiosity rely on loosely-structured processes to ensure inquisitiveness and imaginative thinking so that the inspiring factors such as group variety and team work are mobilised and the impairing ones diminished. Creating, and fostering cultures of curiosity makes demands on a scenario process design. At the epistemological level, interest in the future needs to be stimulated. Analytically, those involved should keep an open mind throughout and avoid a dogmatic adherence to favoured concepts and ideas.

Procedurally, it is important to remember that tools only play a supportive role. If a group is resistant to exploring the future with an open mind, it is unlikely that a tool will make the difference between a good and a bad scenario study. At a contextual level, it is important to nurture those environments that foster independent curiosity-driven research but these appear to be diminishing at present. Curiosity-driven research has traditionally been the province of universities but today they are pressured to work in a more market-oriented manner with fewer opportunities for research that deviates from established paradigms. Cultures of curiosity are not usually found in client-based research because the type of output is often constrained by the desires of the client. Nor are they usual in regulatory institutions whose interest is the optimal functioning of the existing system.

## Some reflections: scenarios for the very long term

To probe beneath the surface of social life to examine deeper processes, it is necessary to investigate the interaction between historical events and the processes which have shaped present-day society and their implications for the future. The classification of time of the 20$^{th}$ century French historian Fernand Braudel (1902-1985) provides a valuable heuristic framework for investigating the interaction of societal events and underlying processes. He (1980) criticised historians and social scientists for their limited appreciation of time in general and long-term developments in particular. Similarly, Slaughter (2002) distinguishes three different levels of operation in future studies: "pop", problem-oriented, and critical and epistemological futures studies. He argues that the first corresponds to the familiar "litany" in the media – population explosion, resources running out, choking pollution, the crime wave. Problem-oriented futures studies involve the more serious exploration of how societies and organisations respond, or should respond, to the near-term future. Critical and epistemological futures studies can probe beneath the surface of social life to examine deeper processes at work. Braudel and Slaughter both argue that their respective disciplines should be looking at more deep-seated societal patterns.

Braudel (1972) offers categorisations of time which distinguish "geographical time" or the *longue durée,* social time, and an individual time or *l'histoire événementielle* (after the economist, Francois Simiand). The *longue durée* refers to fundamental geographic and climatic processes that influence the human race over centuries, even millennia. The long-term processes and cycles of the *longue durée* exert a dominant and stabilising influence over the other levels, providing the context in which other social developments occur. Social time, which includes socio-economic trends such as the Industrial revolution, spans decades or hundreds of years. *L'histoire événementielle* is the traditional approach – the history of events such as battles and elections which span days, weeks, and a number of months. Braudel argued that it is the task of the historian to move beyond the history of events towards a focus on civilisation as a whole. Only then can the meaning of events be fully understood.

A classification such as Braudel's is a useful heuristic or "tool" for the development of meaningful scenarios. His classification might help develop a rigorous theory of why specific changes occur and why they lead to particular outcomes, whereby a bridge is developed between policy choices and outcomes. A comparable categorisation for scenario development is proposed by Van der Heijden's iceberg analysis (1996) which distinguishes between events, trends and patterns, and systemic structure. The top of the iceberg is the level of observable events, while immediately below the water line are trends and patterns. The base of the iceberg is systemic structure, which shapes the levels above it. The iceberg is a whole; the three levels are thus strongly interconnected.

## Conclusion

There are many types of scenario approaches in use at the moment ranging from the highly exploratory to the decision-oriented, and intuitive to analytical. The scenarios that they produce demonstrate varying degrees of complexity. There is no single "correct" approach and different contexts require different scenario approaches. The typology helps to organise the diversity of studies to cut a path through the thicket of possibilities. It helps create an overview of contemporary scenario practice, which might be used to help determine the design of a scenario process. The OECD "Schooling for Tomorrow" project might benefit from the typology by using it to learn from scenario experiences in sectors beyond education. These range from the computer model-oriented approaches used in the environmental community to the brainstorm-type approaches taken in many commercial organisations.

The diversity in scenario approaches makes working with scenarios a flexible approach to exploring the future, which can be shaped to fit different tasks. In the benefits of this flexibility, however, lurks the danger of abuse. Braudel's classification of time might be a useful tool to avoid cosmetic scenarios. However, it is unlikely that a tool can be effective without a genuine interest in considering the future and being prepared to confront flawed assumptions about it. Therefore, beyond focusing on tools, a scenario team would be wise to make efforts to create cultures of curiosity: environments driven by inquisitiveness and imaginative thinking about the future. Such curiosity-driven research, free of vested interests and organisational impediments are likely to do more for free-thinking scenario development than any so-called scenario "tool". Creating and nurturing these cultures ensures that scenario developers are well equipped to embark on Proust's voyages of discovery.

# *References*

Banister, D. *et al.* (2000), *European Transport Policy and Sustainable Mobility*, Spon, London and New York.

Bertrand, G. *et al.* (1999), *Scenarios Europe 2010*, European Commission Forward Studies Unit, Brussels.

Bobbitt, P. (2002), *The Shield of Achilles: War, Peace and the Course of History*, Penguin, London.

Braudel, F. (1972), *The Mediterranean and the Mediterranean World in the Age of Philip II*, Harper and Row, New York.

Braudel, F. (1980), *On History*, Wiedenfeld and Nicolson, London.

Breunesse, E. *et al.* (2000), *Koersen op de toekomst: vier toekomstscenarios voor modern leiderschap* ("Navigating our way to the future: four scenarios for modern leadership"), NIVE.

Brooks, H. (1986), "The Typology of Surprises in Technology, Institutions, and Development", in W.C. Clark and R.E. Munn (eds.), *Sustainable Development of the Biosphere*, Cambridge University Press, Cambridge, UK, pp. 325-350.

CPB Netherlands Bureau for Economic Policy Analysis (1992), *The Netherlands in Triplicate: A Scenario Study of the Dutch Economy* (in Dutch), SDU Uitgeverij, The Hague.

CPB Netherlands Bureau for Economic Policy Analysis (1999), *WorldScan. The Core Version*, CPB Netherlands Bureau for Economic Policy Analysis, The Hague.

Digital Thinking Network (2000), *The Future of Television*, www.dtn.net, accessed May 2001.

Ducot, C. and H.J. Lubben (1980), "A Typology for Scenarios", *Futures*, Vol. 12(1), pp. 15-57.

Duncan, N.E. and P. Wack (1994), "Scenarios Designed to Improve Decision Making", *Planning Review*, Vol. 22(4), pp. 18-25, 46.

European Environment Agency (1999), *Environment in the European Union at the Turn of the Century*, European Environment Agency, Copenhaguen.

European Environment Agency and ICIS (2000), *Cloudy Crystal Balls: An Assessment of Recent European and Global Scenario Studies and Models*.

Fuller, T. *et al.* (2003), "Entrepreneurial Foresight; A Case Study in Reflexivity, Experiments, Sensitivity and Reorganisation", in H. Tsoukas and J. Shepherd (eds.), *Developing Strategic Foresight in the Knowedge Economy: Probing the Future*, Blackwell, Oxford.

Gertner, R. and M. Knez (2000), "Speltheorie in de realiteit" ("Game theory in reality"), *Het Financieele Dagblad*, pp. 12-13.

Global Business Network (1998), "Destino Colombia", *Deeper News*, No. 9.

Godet, M. (1997), *Scenarios and Strategies: A Toolbox for Scenario Planning*, Conservatoire National des Arts et Métiers (CNAM).

Godet, M. and F. Roubelat (1996), "Creating the Future: The Use and Misuse of Scenarios", *Long Range Planning*, Vol. 29(2), pp. 164-171.

Goffman, E. (1959), *The Presentation of Self in Every Day Life*, Doubleday Anchor Books.

Hammond, A. (1998), *Which World? Scenarios for the 21st Century. Global Destinies, Regional Choices*, Earthscan Publications Ltd, London.

van der Heijden, K. (1996), *Scenarios: the Art of Strategic Conversation*, Wiley, Chichester.

van der Heijden, K. *et al.* (2002), *The Sixth Sense: Accelerating Organisational Learning with Scenarios*, Wiley & Sons, Chichester.

Heugens, P.M.A.R. and J. Van Oosterhout (2001), "To Boldly Where No Man Has Gone Before: Integrating Cognitive and Physical Features in Scenario Studies", *Futures*, Vol. 33(10), pp. 861-872.

Intergovernmental Panel on Climate Change (2000), "Emissions Scenarios", Cambridge University Press, Cambridge.

de Jong, R. (1998), "De geschiedenis van de toekomst: De ontwikkeling van vier scenarios voor intemediairs op de arbeidsmarkt van 2010" ("The history of the future: the development of four scenarios for intermediaries on the job market in 2010"), Faculteit Bedrijfskunde, University of Groningen, Groningen.

Kahane, A. (1998), "Imagining South Africa's Future: How Scenarios Helped Discover Common Ground", in L. Fahey and R. Randall, *Learning from the Future: Competitive Foresight Scenarios*, John Wiley & Sons, New York.

Masini, E.B. and J.M. Vasquez (2000), "Scenarios as Seen from a Human and Social Perspective", *Technological Forecasting and Social Change*, Vol. 65, pp. 49-66.

McCorduck, P. and N. Ramsey (1996), *The Futures of Women: Scenarios for the 21st Century*, Warner Books, New York.

McKiernan, P. *et al.* (2001a), "Scenarios for Scotland", *Scenario and Strategy Planning*, 2.

McKiernan, P. *et al.* (2001b), "The Low Road. Scenarios for Scotland Part II", *Scenario and Strategy Planning*, 2.

McKiernan, P. *et al.* (2001c), "The High Road", *Scenario and Strategy Planning*, 3.

McRae, H. (1995), *The World in 2020: Power, Culture and Prosperity. A Vision of the Future*, Harper Collins, London.

Morgan, D. (2002), "Images of the Future: A Historical Perspective", *Futures*, Vol. 34(9/10), pp. 883-893.

Moyer, K. (1996), "Scenario Planning at British Airways – A Case Study", *Long Range Planning*, Vol. 29, pp. 172-181.

Nakamae, T. (1998), "Three Futures for Japan: Views from 2020", *The Economist*, March 21.

Netherlands Scientific Council for Government Policy (WRR) (1994), *Sustained Risks: A Lasting Phenomenon*, SDU Uitgeverij, The Hague.

van Notten, Ph.W.F. (2000), "Create the Future: 21-22 June Workshop Report", ICIS, Maastricht.

van Notten, Ph.W.F. (2005), "Writing on the Wall: Scenario Development in Times of Discontinuity", *Dissertation*, www.dissertation.com

OECD (1997), *The World in 2020. Towards a New Global Age*, OECD, Paris.

Postma, T.J.B.M. et al. (1995), "Toekomstverkenning met scenario's: Een hulpmiddel bij de bepaling van de strategische koers van een organisatie" ("Foresight using scenarios: an aid in determining the strategy of an organization"), *Bedrijfskunde*, Vol. 2, pp. 13-19.

Ringland, G. (1998), *Scenario Planning*, John Wiley & Sons, Chichester.

Robinson, J. (1990), "Futures under Glass: A Recipe for People who Hate to Predict", *Futures*, Vol. 22(8), pp. 820-842.

Rorsch, A. and C. de Hart (1993), *Threshold 2000: Constraints and Scenarios for Sustainable Development in the Netherlands and Europe*, Elmar Rijswijk, Rijswijk.

Rotmans, J. and H.J.M. de Vries (1997), *Perspectives on Global Change: The TARGETS Approach*, Cambridge University Press, Cambridge.

Rotmans, J. et al. (2000), "Visions for a Sustainable Europe", *Futures*, Vol. 32(9-10), pp. 809-831.

Schoemaker, P.J.H. (1995), "Scenario Planning: A Tool for Strategic Thinking", *Sloan Management Review* (Winter), pp. 25-39.

Schoemaker, P.J.H. (1998), "Twenty Common Pitfalls in Scenario Planning", in L. Fahey and R. M. Randall (eds.), *Learning from the Future: Competitive Foresight Scenarios*, John Wiley & Sons, New York, pp. 422-431.

Schwartz, P. (1991), *The Art of the Long View: Planning for the Future in an Uncertain World*, Currency Doubleday, New York.

Schwartz, P. et al. (1999), *The Long Boom: A Vision for the Coming Age of Prosperity*, Perseus, Boulder.

Shell International (2002), *People and Connections: Global Scenarios to 2020 – Public Summary*, London.

Slaughter, R.A. (2002), "Beyond the Mundane: Reconciling Breadth and Depth in Futures Enquiry", *Futures*, Vol. 34(6), pp. 493-507.

Sparrow, O. (2000), "Making Use of Scenarios – From the Vague to the Concrete", *Scenario & Strategy Planning*, Vol. 2(5), pp. 18-21.

van Steenbergen, B. (2003), "De Nieuwe Mens in de Toekomstige Wereldmaatschappij: Uitdagingen voor de Toekomstonderzoeker" ("The new human in the future world society: challenges for the futures researcher"), Nyenrode University, Breukelen.

Stuurgroep Toekomstonderzoek en Strategisch Omgevingsbeleid (2000), *Terugblik op toekomstverkenningen* ("A retrospective look at foresight studies"), Netherlands Scientific Council for Government Policy (WRR), The Hague.

UNEP (2002), *Global Environment Outlook 3: Past, Present and Future Perspectives*, Earthscan, London.

Van't Klooster, S.A. and M.B.A. van Asselt (2006), "Practicing the Scenario-Axes Technique", *Futures*, Vol. 38(1), pp. 15-30.

Wack, P. (1985), "Scenarios: Uncharted Waters Ahead", *Harvard Business Review*, Vol. 63(5), pp. 72-79.

Wilson, I. (2000), "From Scenario Thinking to Strategic Action", *Technological Forecasting & Social Change*, Vol. 65, pp. 23-29.

World Business Council for Sustainable Development (1998), *Exploring Sustainable Development. Global scenarios 2000-2050*, WBCSD, London.

World Business Council for Sustainable Development (2000), "Biotechnology Scenarios", Conches-Geneva.

# Chapter 5
# Futures studies, scenarios, and the "possibility-space" approach

by
Riel Miller[1]

*Riel Miller presents the field of futures studies, drawing a number of parallels with the study of history. He describes how the search for greater predictive accuracy involves risks. One is of adopting forecasting methods and models that depend too heavily on what happened in the past as if the future could be extrapolated; another is that preoccupation with what is likely to happen can obscure consideration of other futures which may be less likely but still possible and potentially more desirable. He discusses "trend-based" scenarios and "preference-based" scenarios as liable to such limitations, which limitations can impair strategic decision making. He presents the "possibility-space" approach as an alternative to them.*

## Thinking rigorously about the future

People think about the future all the time – in the morning when they wake-up and start planning the day ahead, at the dinner table when they discuss where to go on vacation, or which university the children should attend, or what will happen to the stock market. Most of these reflections are short-term, a few hours, days or months. Such conversations naturally mix together what people hope for with a wide range of expectations – from the probable to the improbable. Degrees of probability are handled more

---

[1] Associate, Demos, London and Senior Visiting Fellow, Danish Technological Institute.

carefully by professional forecasters trying to predict tomorrow's weather or next year's economic growth. Professionals tend to focus on getting to the highest probability prediction that available data and models can provide. They generally steer away from considering the broader, less predictive question of what might be possible, as well as from the more normative question of what is desirable.

But the search for greater predictive accuracy involves certain trade-offs. On the one hand, there is a risk of adopting forecasting methods and models that depend too heavily on what happened in the past. Yesterday's parameters may do a good job of tracking past events but experience shows that this approach consistently misses major inflection points and transformative changes. On the other hand, a preoccupation with what is likely to happen tends to obscure things that may be unlikely but still possible and potentially more desirable. At best, the safety of extrapolation ignores what is not predictable; at worst it lulls us into a false sense of having exhausted the available options, thereby narrowing the set of available choices. This, in turn, can impair strategic decision making because it limits the capacity to imagine non-predictable ends and means. The "possibility-space" approach outlined in this chapter offers one avenue for overcoming such constraints.

## *What is futures studies?*

Broad socio-economic changes are propelling the development of futures thinking. Compared to well-established academic disciplines, like economics, futures studies lack a coherent and widely accepted foundation. Most economists generally agree, after some two centuries of heated debate, that economics is the study of the allocation of scarce resources. The analyses of today's orthodox micro, macro, public, short-run, long-run, econometric and historical economists overwhelmingly originate in the root question – how do we allocate scarce resources?

Of course economics was not born a full-grown discipline. Nor at the outset was there much consensus regarding the fundamental analytical problem that connected all of the far-flung issues and theories that now fall under the rubric: mainstream economics. Adam Smith, arguably the founder of economics as a discipline, studied and taught moral philosophy and *"belles lettres"*. Over time, however, economics evolved into an academic discipline driven by the development of markets and industry, the shift to generalised wage labour and the rise of highly complex and diversified systems for allocating resources. It developed into a field that addressed the analytical challenges posed by the increasing intricacy and ever growing variety of actually functioning markets.

In a similar fashion, the emergence of futures studies is closely linked to the growing complexity, diversity and freedom (or indeterminacy) that characterises today's answers to an equally fundamental question: how might we reproduce daily life in the future?[2] Futures studies is being pulled by, and to a certain extent helping to propel, an explosion in the plausible although not necessarily either the probable or desirable – permutations of the ways in which everyday life is reproduced. In terms of how we live our lives, the daily question – what do I do now? – is becoming more open. It is this possibility of a future with greater freedom that calls for the development of more systematic and refined tools for thinking about the future.

What distinguishes futures studies from other disciplines is their preoccupation with how we create the future everyday and on this basis to analyse the prospects for change – be it one day or a century from now. This approach to thinking about the future contrasts markedly with more traditional and familiar modes like mystical prophecy, grand ideologically-inspired utopias and mechanistic predictive models. Not that horoscopes, messianic visions or efforts at building the perfect model will disappear. The yearning for predictive certainty responds to other needs. Those who are certain that human history will end with the coming of the Messiah or decide what clothes to wear because Jupiter is aligned with Mars are certainly thinking about the future. But they are seeking the opposite of what future studies are about. Most of futures studies focus on exposing how the future cannot be predicted because it is contingent on choices we make starting now. The aim is to evoke a much wider and deeper set of possible futures, in this sense entirely unlike the predictive traditions that depend very heavily on either continuity or on exogenous events like an apocalypse.

There is one part of future studies that *is* interested in short-term prediction, using empirical models. These studies look at situations where the inertia of the immediate past can be reasonably expected to restrict the degree of possible change. Short-run predictive models can be important when they provide insights into the specific variables (forces) that reproduce daily life – or that slice of daily life that interests the forecaster. Done properly, a forecast offers understanding of the causal factors that change

---

[2] North (1999) addressing the question "What are the limits to our understanding of the world around us?", suggests that gaining this understanding depends largely on addressing uncertainty. He proposes three kinds of uncertainty: uncertainty due to insufficient information and knowledge; uncertainty due to the fact that the world is non-ergodic – *i.e.* is undergoing continuous change; and uncertainty arising from the lack of adequate theories of continuous change.

daily life, of the way the different variables interact, and of how far the past is a good basis for looking into the future. But when forecasting bumps into the limits of its effective range, it provides a clear signal that efforts at prediction must give way to an exploration of what might be possible, before jumping into assessments of what and why particular outcomes are more or less probable.

## *Futures studies and history*

Thus, the distinctiveness of future studies is in providing a rigorous approach to the plausibility of different configurations for the reproduction of daily life in the future. This task parallels those of the historian seeking to understand the key factors that altered (or not) daily life in the past, be it the decisions of kings, the outcome of wars, or the composition of peasant meals (Hawthorn, 1991, p. 8). Neither the historian nor the futurist has direct access to the reality they are analysing. Both futurists and historians seek clues in the present and the past in order to substantiate their analyses of why and how life did or might unfold, using methods and theories that take into account multiple layers of complex interaction and causality. Like history, futures studies are a polyvalent, neutral "social science" as it is a collection of methods, theories and findings that provides an analytical tool for people who hold different beliefs and goals (see for example: Booth *et al.*, 2004; Dator, 2002; Godet, 2001a and b; Keenan *et al.*, 2003; Ogilvy, 2002; Ringland, 2002; Van der Heijden, 2002).

There are, of course, some important contrasts. The work of a futurist may be tested one day by the arrival of tomorrow, while the historian must be forever content with the traces of the past that are more or less buried under the weight of time. Historians can consult the historical record to show definitively that a treaty was signed while futurists must use their imaginations to map what might be the global agreement of tomorrow. But both are map makers – trying to extract the essential features that may explain how life was, or will be lived. In many cases historians can track detailed records far into the past with considerable reliability, whereas futurists are more preoccupied with the seeds of tomorrow scattered in the overwhelming detail of the present. However, the challenge of developing convincing analyses of how daily life was or will be reproduced remains the same (Bruland, 2001).

Futures studies and history share five key axioms. First, whether looking to the past or the future, as the analysis moves farther away from the present uncertainty increases across a number of dimensions and the accuracy with which we can explain how a particular aspect of daily life is reproduced diminishes. In part this is because the quality of the raw data declines and in part because the number of potential sources or causes that might account for change (or stasis) is, in most circumstances, bound to grow over time.

The second joint axiom is that the scale and pace of change need to be evaluated in both absolute and relative terms. Everyone knows that change from a very low base can be quite small in absolute terms but huge relative to the starting point or when the starting point is already large even a big absolute change may be small in relative terms. A good example of this is the projected population changes for India, which starts from a base of over 1 billion. As a result, despite a slower recent growth rate, India's total population in 2050 could be 500 million higher than in 2000 – overtaking China.[3]

The third axiom is that over time, whether looking backwards or forwards, many of the metrics and benchmarks we use to assess change also change. Not so long ago the metric for speed was not miles or kilometres per hour but the speed of a horse measured in furlongs – 1/8 of a mile. When it comes to benchmarks, the old Model T Ford was considered dangerous at over 45 mph. Today most cars are safe at much higher speeds. Judging speed today using the metrics and benchmarks of the equestrian or Model T eras makes no sense.

Fourth, and even trickier to detect and apply, are the more subjective, capacity-related shifts. The relevance and calibration of different measures and perceptions of events in daily life are shaped by a whole range of factors like the degree of literacy, the extent to which values are shared within the community, and the ease of access to information. Even if we are aware of these factors they make comparisons over time difficult. For instance, can we compare the widespread fear of nuclear war in the 1960s to people's fear of genetically modified organisms in the first decade of the 21st century?

There is a fifth axiom to bring the abstract potential for infinite variation down to a manageable range. In order to reduce the "degrees of freedom" in interpreting the past or imagining the future we turn to the facts and reasonable assumptions that restrict what is possible. First assumptions have to be made about uncertainly (the first axiom). Aliens could land on Earth tomorrow or we could be hit by an extinction scale meteor and all efforts to imagine future possibilities would be rendered moot and null. Futurists,

---

[3] The United Nations Estimates World Population Prospects 1950-2050 (The 2002 Revision), February 2003, shows that in the medium variant India's rate of population growth falls from an average of around 2% in the latter half of the 20th century to under 1% on average for the first half of the 21st century. However the total growth is close to 500 million.

particularly those interested in policy issues, do not need to devote too much attention to this kind of uncertainty since, though such exogenous events might happen, there is nothing much to say right now about the day after.

As for axioms two, three and four, absolute, relative and qualitative changes are all constrained, often in different ways, but nevertheless limited by key attributes of the physical, social and intellectual world. The average height and life-span of the human population may change, even rapidly, but within fairly important limits. Similarly in the realm of social organisation, be it economic, political or sociological, we assume that the range of options is relatively limited. Looking at societal change over the next 30 years it is probable that politics will be bounded on the range from despotism to democracy, economics from plan to market and social identity from undifferentiated to differentiated, with the long-run trend in all fields towards the latter ends of the spectrum. The strand of time that most historians and futurists usually consider exhibits a degree of continuity that makes meaningful analysis possible.

However, that the "degrees of freedom" of possible changes are within a manageable range for the purposes of in-depth analysis does not resolve in any way which particular methods or theories historians or futurists should use for such an analysis and here the choices remain very wide, with historians and futurists mostly going their separate ways. Futurists have a well established tool kit for developing scenarios, examining trends and polling expert opinion (see de Jouvenel, 2004; Ogilvy, 2002). The products of these analyses are used for a variety of purposes – from simply adding to the stock of knowledge to helping make action-oriented strategic decisions. However, as is to be expected in a field that is still young and evolving rapidly, innovations and debates about basic methods and goals still reign.

## Trend- and preference-based scenarios

Scenarios or stories about distinct futures have the potential to overcome some of the pitfalls of predictive approaches. What scenarios lose in terms of calibrated probabilistic accuracy can be made up for by a greater openness to initially unlikely but nevertheless possible outcomes. This is why scenarios have often been used as a tool for strategic thinking, "strategic" in the sense of choosing where to go. The strategic choices involve the selection of overarching, sometimes long-run, goals. And strategic choices are the ones that make a significant difference in the direction of travel, towards or away from strategic goals. Scenarios are also well suited to helping decision makers think about institutional change. However, scenarios face a number of drawbacks, in particular how to imagine and then select a few distinctive and pertinent stories about the long-term future from among the infinite number that is possible.

There are two familiar methods for solving the problem of how to choose scenarios. The first takes an initial starting point, for instance population or economic output, and then develops scenarios on the basis of a range of growth rates – low, medium and high – or trends (I call this the "baby bear, mama bear and papa bear" approach, or "Bear" for short.) The second approach focuses more on preferences and implicit expectations in order to sketch scenarios that capture what people consider to be: the most desirable, the least desirable, and the muddling through but most likely (I call this the GBU approach: good, bad and ugly.) Both of these methods have the virtue of selecting stories that are readily accessible since the factors that determine the main characteristics of each scenario are usually quite familiar and easy to grasp. We are well acquainted with trend scenarios for universities, for instance, that are distinguished by differences in enrolment growth rates or scenarios distinguished by the preferences that lead people to consider the "good" scenario to be one where universities are exclusively citadels of a pure search for knowledge, the "bad" scenario to be one where universities are exclusively driven by the commercial imperatives of funders from the private sector, and a muddling through or "ugly" scenario, usually seen as the most likely, to be one that combines both pure and commercial options.

## The limitations of trend- and preference-based scenarios

Exercises based both on trends and values are generally empowering – giving participants a sense of perspective and reminding them of the potential for change (moving beyond current conflicts, zero-sum games, going over or around the wall instead of through it, etc.). They are useful empowerment techniques for promoting leadership. But both suffer from drawbacks that limit the utility of the stories.

The first problem *is the risk of narrowness and lack of imagination*. This is not an absolute characteristic as trends and preferences can be taken "far out", becoming highly imaginative (usually "unrealistic" too). However, these types of stories too often remain circumscribed by initial perceptions of trends and preferences. This may be compounded by the "hubris of the now": "I am alive now and everything is more difficult (or easier), faster (or slower), bigger (or smaller) than in the old days." This view fails to put trends and current views of the present in an historical perspective. Trend-based scenarios also narrow down the range of possibilities when the trends are identified not in terms of theories of change and hypotheses regarding causality but simply on the basis of already available data. Starting with given trends and preferences makes it harder to take into account the compound, multi-dimensional nature of change. Change alters what is possible. A literate population can do things that were very difficult to imagine when the population was illiterate; the options open to a child are not the same as those of an adult – over time not only what a person can do, but what they want to do changes.

The second major limitation *is a lack of analytical precision.* Because the trends and preferences are usually taken as self-evident, even if the effort is made to quantify, categorise and mix the different elements of each story, the theoretical models of change (*i.e.* of causal inter-action) are most often not well developed. Lacking developed theories of change and charged with an overabundance of descriptive detail, it becomes difficult not only to extract analytically distinguishable stories but more crucially from a policy perspective to justify any particular selection of stories from amongst the vast possible range. Certainly Bear and GBU processes generate stories, in abundance, but such scenarios are usually of limited value for policy-making because of a lack of analytical foundations. So, the question becomes, is there a way to develop scenarios that expands the range of imaginable possibilities and that promises to improve analytical clarity in thinking about the future?

## Possibility-space scenarios

Partial coverage of the full set of possible futures is inevitable as we cannot imagine every feasible outcome. Figure 5.1 illustrates the challenge. The largest set consists of what is possible. Within the set of possibilities are all probable futures and some of the desirable ones. Since desirability is in the eye of the beholder this set contains both good and bad scenarios and there are some desirable futures that do not fall within the realm of the possible. The preference-based scenarios are located within the set of desirable/undesirable possibilities while the scenarios based on trend extrapolations may be found across the possible, desirable and impossible futures. As these do not necessarily cover the full range of pertinent possibilities, are there methods to improve our exploration of the strategically-relevant range of possible futures?

# CHAPTER 5. FUTURES STUDIES, SCENARIOS, AND THE "POSSIBILITY-SPACE" APPROACH – 101

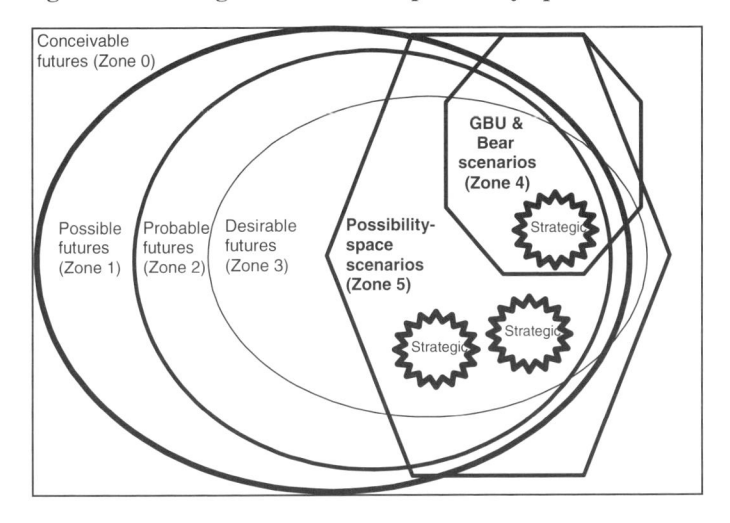

**Figure 5.1. Strategic scenarios and possibility-space futures**

*Source*: Author.

The "possibility-space" approach elaborated below offers one way of generating a larger set of possible futures for consideration in scenario building through a three-step method. The first step is to determine or define the key attribute (variable A) of the scenario's subject. The second step is to sketch a space, perhaps multidimensional, using the primary attributes of change (a, b, c) in variable A. The third step is to identify distinct scenarios within the possibility space. Figure 5.2 illustrates this approach with a technological example of the pervasiveness of electricity. The three steps for arriving at this possibility space are as follows:

- *Step 1:* The subject of the scenario is technology pervasiveness (variable A), defined in terms of how widely a particular technology is diffused. When a technology is first invented or commercialised it is possible that it will not be picked up at all. Alternatively it might become very widely diffused, entering all aspects of life – from the workplace to the home.

- *Step 2:* Two of the key attributes of technology's pervasiveness are a) how easy it is to use, and b) to how many uses it can be put. As electricity becomes easier to use and is applied to more different uses, it moves from the lower left quadrant of the possibility space to the upper right.

- *Step 3:* Different scenarios can be developed by considering different points in the possibility space. We already know what has happened to electricity but we do not know what is going to happen to many more recent technological breakthroughs. Will information technology, for instance, really succeed in becoming as easy to use and ambient as electricity?

**Figure 5.2. Possibility-space illustration – pervasiveness of electricity**

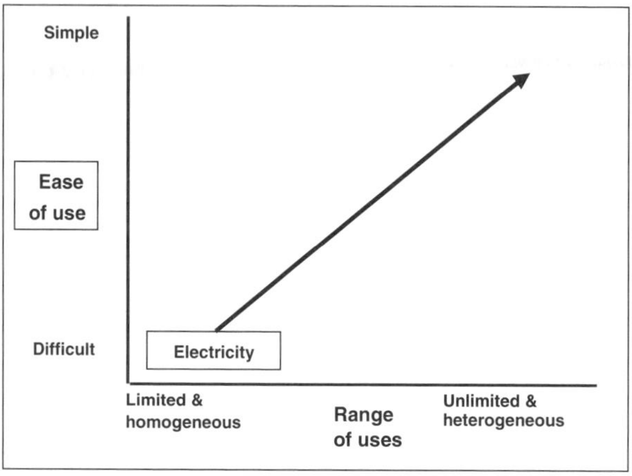

*Source*: Author.

## *Extracting scenarios from possibilities – a functionalist approach*

Having enlarged the set of available possible futures for consideration when developing scenarios, the next challenge is to select particular scenarios from the vast space of possibilities. There are still the trend and preference approaches that could be applied immediately to the broader set of possibilities, as the basis for selecting from within the larger possibility space, either by taking the starting point and rates of change as givens or by imposing a specific set of values for differentiating end-points. Or, we may put off consideration of probabilities and preferences and continue for one more step with the neutrality of the possibility-space methodology by focusing on the functions and/or organisational attributes of the scenarios subject. Continuing with the example of electricity, imagine it as a technology that has not yet traced its path across time (see a discussion of counter-factuals in Booth, 2004). In the example used here there are three hypothetical functions and two basic organisational patterns that can be used to develop scenarios as per Table 5.1. The three imaginary functions of electrical power are as: i) weapon/tool of war; ii) local replacement for steam and water power in factories; and iii) autonomous power source for all kinds of consumer products. The two organisational attributes are centralised and decentralised generation of electrical power. This imaginary "what-if" of the future of electricity generates six scenarios.

**Table 5.1. Organisation and function scenarios for "what-if" electricity use scenarios**

| Function | Organisation | |
|---|---|---|
| | Centralised generation | Decentralised generation |
| Weapon | Scenario 1 | Scenario 2 |
| Industrial power | Scenario 3 | Scenario 4 |
| Consumer power | Scenario 5 | Scenario 6 |

*Source*: Author.

Figure 5.3 shows the six scenarios mapped in a very approximate way onto the possibility space already depicted by Figure 5.2. This step underscores the contingency or dependency of the scenario's subject – the pervasiveness of electricity (variable A) – on changes in the underlying attributes of change [ease-of-use (a) and range of uses (b)], that are then used to locate particular scenarios within the possibility space.

**Figure 5.3. Examples of functional technology scenarios**

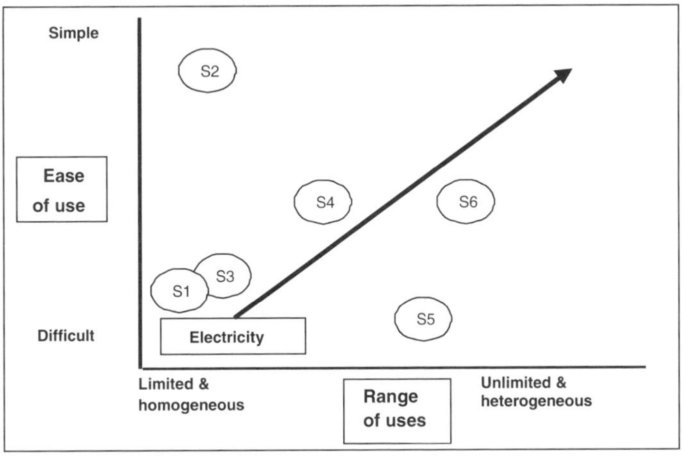

*Source*: Author.

Figure 5.3 shows scenarios S2, S4 and S6 mapped higher on the scale of ease-of-use on the grounds that decentralised generation implies a reduction in the technical difficulties of using power generation technologies (wind, solar, hydrogen, etc.). Scenarios S4, S5 and S6 are deemed to exhibit a wider range of uses since as a decentralised tool for industry (S4) and a general tool for consumers (S5, S6), electricity is bound to be used in many different ways. In S1, where electricity is held exclusively by the military as a specialised weapon dependent on the centralised generation of power there would be little need to develop ease-of-use for either generation or applications, while the range of uses is very narrow. Hence S1 is in the lower left of the possibility space. Similarly S3 is closer to the lower left since big industry does its best to limit diffusion.

Electricity did not follow any of these scenarios since it diffused across all three functions and the ease-of-use problems on the application side were largely solved through centralised provision of electric current. Today electricity is located closer to the lower right quadrant, if ease-of-use is considered a composite indicator of both generation and application. Using this electricity pervasiveness possibility space to imagine a different outcome means, for instance, considering what it would take to get to the upper-right quadrant. Such an analysis would focus on a story where universal access and application is combined with simple decentralised power generators. This scenario might be chosen because people value highly universal access and application as well as local control. Or because there is a hypothesis that easy-to-use decentralised generation might allow for innovations in the spatial and temporal organisation of daily life.

Having determined that the scenario in the upper-right corresponds with people's values the next step is to analyse the attributes and conditions for the realisation of such a scenario. This takes us to the final step in the strategic possibility-space approach. The analysis now moves to estimating probability on the basis of assessments of how likely or not the choices deemed necessary to get to the goal will be chosen and effectively implemented. Choices have been defined by pushing the realm of the possible on the basis of clear analytical models. In this way decision making, the core of democracy, and the specific policies that are meant to follow through on democratic choices, come to the forefront.

These illustrations show how the possibility-space method opens up a wider set of possibilities for constructing scenarios. The possibility space creates an alternative range of options from which to construct strategic scenarios, by exploring the future more independently of initial views regarding probability and desirability. The task is still one of imagining the future – projecting forward into time. Possibility spaces make it easier to be imaginative, systematic and explicit about the hypothetical "what if". Modelling can help analyse which variables matter and, once the possibilities have been rigorously explored, modelling can be an important tool for deepening the analysis of the factors that might influence rates and directions of change as we have explored in moving towards quantifying a possibility-space scenario for the learning society (Miller and Bentley, 2003).

# *References*

Booth, C., P. Clark, A. Delahaye, M. Rowlinson and S. Proctor (2004), "How Modal Narratives Work".

Bruland, K. (2001), "Technological Revolutions, Innovation Systems and Convergence from a Historical Perspective", University of Oslo, February.

Dator, J. (2002), *Advancing Futures*, Prager.

Godet, M. (2001a), *Creating Futures: Scenario Planning as a Strategic Management Tool*, Economica.

Godet, M. (2001b), *Manuel de prospective stratégique*, Dunod.

Hawthorn, G. (1991), "Plausible Worlds: Possibility and Understanding in History and the Social Sciences", Cambridge University Press.

van der Heijden, K. (2002), *The Sixth Sense: Accelerating Organizational Learning with Scenarios*, John Wiley & Sons.

de Jouvenel, H. (2004), "An Invitation to Foresight", *Futuribles*.

Keenan, M., D. Abbott, F. Scapolo and M. Zappacosta (2003), *Mapping Foresight Competence in Europe: The Eurofore Pilot Project*, IPTS, June.

Miller, R. and T. Bentley (2003), "Unique Creation – Possible Futures – Four Scenarios for 21st Century Schooling", NCSL, Nottingham.

North, D.C. (1999), "Dealing with a Non-ergodic world: Institutional Economics, Property Rights and the Global Environment", Duke Environmental Law and Policy Forum, Fall, Vol. X, No. 1, pp. 1-12, *www.law.duke.edu/shell/cite.pl?10+Duke+Envtl.+L.+&+Pol'y+F.+1*

Ogilvy, J.A. (2002), *Creating Better Futures: Scenario Planning as a Tool for a Better Tomorrow*, Oxford University Press.

Ringland, G. (2002), *Scenarios in Public Policy*, John Wiley & Sons.

# Chapter 6
# Futures thinking methodologies and options for education

by
Jonas Svava Iversen[1]

*This chapter by Jonas Svava Iversen gives a user-oriented view of a range of scenario methodologies. The author presents scenarios as involving four phases, and elaborates each in terms of their purpose, techniques to achieve them, and insights about successful practice and potential pitfalls. i) Mapping and delineation of the subject matter is a critical first step. ii) Identification of critical issues and trends is the second, and this is divided into analytical and participatory methods. iii) Creating scenarios is itself sub-divided into five: identification of drivers, consolidation of trends, prioritisation of trends, identification of scenario axes, and actor analysis. The fourth step, iv) using scenarios, looks at three main uses: developing shared knowledge, strengthening public discourse, and supporting decisions.*

## Delineation and mapping

It is important to establish what exactly the scenario is going to be used for, which processes will be used, and which level of complexity is chosen[2] (*i.e.* delineating). This calls for a first overview of the most salient elements in the area on which the scenarios will focus, *i.e.* a mapping exercise. Delineating and mapping sets the ground for the rest of the work, giving

---

[1] Senior Consultant, Policy Analysis and Innovation, Danish Technological Institute.

[2] This delineation is based on the discussion in the chapter by Van Notten (Chapter 4).

focus to the identification of trends and issues and the building of scenarios, and helping to ensure that design is thought through and not missing important elements.

## *Delineation*

"Delineating" means making choices about the goals and processes of the scenario analysis, where decisions related to goals influence decisions related to processes and *vice versa*. The choice of design should be based on an evaluation of the goal of the process, the capacity and the "work-culture" of the participants involved, and the context in which the scenarios are going to be used and disseminated.

The goal of scenario analysis in a policy context may be positioned between the poles of *exploration* and *pre-policy* research. Exploration is traditionally the most common objective of scenario work. Scenarios may be used to explore a wide range of areas, from certain macro trends to particular subjects of interest in an area of policy. Exploration primarily uses scenarios as a vehicle of learning rather than a tool for decision making. Pre-policy research also involves exploration but is at the same time directed at serving more specific policy-oriented goals. This range of purpose means that the study design must incorporate different methods for bringing the scenarios into a strategic and decision-oriented framework.

The analytical design of a scenario process may call more on analytical approaches (convergent thinking) or on intuitive approaches (divergent thinking). Convergent thinking, on the one hand, is essentially about traditional problem solving. It typically involves bringing material from a variety of sources to bear on a problem, in such a way as to produce the "correct" answer. This kind of thinking is particularly appropriate in science and technology, and it involves description, observation, deduction, and/or prioritisation. Divergent thinking, on the other hand, is a skill broadly related to the creative elaboration of ideas prompted by a stimulus. Conventionally, such thinking is regarded as more suited to artistic pursuits and studies within the humanities.

The mix of convergent and divergent thinking found in any scenario study is related to such issues as the use of qualitative vs. quantitative data; participatory vs. model-based scenario design; and inclusive vs. exclusive approach to the identification of the participants in the participatory processes. Scenario analysis may be very simple through to being quite complex. Scenarios used for pre-policy research tend to be less intuitive and more complex than those for exploration.

## *Mapping*

While delineation is related to the goals and design of the scenario process, "mapping" is about establishing an overview of the subject matter. This may be done with the help of desk research, interviews and relevance trees. *Desk research* should involve a wide variety of sources. The Internet is an obvious tool for this and good sources of information are government agencies, non-governmental organisations, international consultancy companies, research communities, and on-line and off-line journals related to the subject. This research may also be used for the identification of experts for the various forms of interviews and participatory processes that may be used during the scenario analysis. In this phase of scenario projects, *interviews* should be with experts with a broad knowledge of the subject matter, since the aim is the mapping and general description of the subject under analysis. Creating *relevance trees* is like mind-mapping and may be useful to understand how a given subject relates to other similar subjects, and they may also be used to help identify the scenario team's knowledge of the different subjects.

## Identification of critical issues and trends

### *Data analysis*

On any subject, there will be a range of information which may be transformed into interesting insights on trends and issues. Methods for these types of analysis draw from different scientific fields.

*Biblio-metric analysis* may be used to track the development of the interest in a given subject and as such it may act as a trend indicator. But there may be other benefits from such form of analysis. An integral part of the biblio-metric approach is an "actor" analysis where the main experts in a given field can be mapped out and called on later in the scenario exercise. The success of any biblio-metric analysis is strongly connected to the identification and use of key search terms.

Extrapolation of historical trends or theorems may also inspire the assessment of different possible developments. As a "rule of thumb", the uptake of technologies, products, and ideas in particular markets and society follow S-curves rather than developing in a linear pattern. This means that uptake or participation will be slow in the beginning but at a certain state tend to reach an almost exponential growth rate before the concept "matures" and the growth stops. On this view, the challenge is to estimate the nature of and location on such an S-curve.

The potential use and development of technology is often an important driver of change in scenario analysis. One way of analysing this quantitatively is to conduct *patent analysis,* since the patterns of patents help indicate the potential interest and breakthrough of technology. Good patent analysis may be an important quantitative input to a scenario analysis and there is range of patent analysis services and tools available. There are, however, at least three pitfalls to note. First, companies may use patents as a strategic tool to discourage other companies from doing research in a given technological field so it is not objective. Second, there is a "black box" effect, since patents only become public some time after they have been filed. Third, patent research may be very time-consuming if knowledge is needed on a very specific technology, since every patent needs close study to understand the specifics of a given patent.

*Participatory methods*

Although desk research and data analysis are very useful, experts will often help provide insights and new perspectives on a subject. The input of experts and stakeholders is thus of key importance to a successful scenario analysis. Identifying the right experts may well present a challenge. Experts with different perspectives and backgrounds may well be needed, as with different stakeholder perspectives.

Once the experts have been identified, their views may be sought face to face, via telephone, or in focus groups, and this may be through structured, semi-structured, or unstructured interviews. Face-to-face interviews should be used for key experts and stakeholders, allowing the interviewer to interpret body language and other "secondary" sources of information. Most often, face-to-face interviews will be semi-structured in order to facilitate the unfolding of a natural conversation kept within certain boundaries by the interview guideline. Telephone interviews are the obvious solution when resources are unavailable to conduct face-to-face interviews. Focus groups can be a very effective way of gaining input from a range of different experts and stakeholders at the same time. Most focus groups are conducted on the basis of a set of questions that are addressed in a relatively unmoderated discussion by the participants.

Although it is often described as if it were an alternative methodology to scenario development, a *Delphi analysis* may be used as the basis for a scenario process. Delphi analysis is a structured brainstorming process carried out iteratively through rounds, usually two to four, of semi-structured questionnaires. A range of experts is asked for their input on a given subject, and through the iteration of questionnaires each is confronted with the inputs of the others. They are then asked to evaluate responses of the other experts and restate any of their initial responses. This process is intended to lead to consensus among the experts involved. *Consensus conferences* are a form of real-time Delphi analysis where the method requires that participants come to agreement on a complex question. Different parties are allowed to state their case, but at the end of the day a degree of consensus must be reached. If this cannot be achieved through discussion, a vote may be taken to give a tangible result.

The public may be involved through the same methods as experts but it should be noted that Delphi analysis is intended for experts and may not extend very constructively to the public. Face-to-face interviews and telephone interviews are very resource-demanding and are often reserved for experts, while the opinions of members of the public may be most effectively introduced via focus groups and questionnaires.

## Scenario creation

The purpose of this phase is to develop a set of internally consistent scenarios. Scenarios may be developed and used in either a normative or an exploratory manner. Normative scenarios are like visions for the future. Often only one or two scenarios need to be developed, and their main purpose is to identify the "perfect future" for a given subject. The scenarios may then be used as a tool to identify actions to be taken by different actors if these visions for the future are to be realised. This method is most often used by organisations which have a very clear political agenda and a set of goals they wish to pursue without too much debate on the uncertainties of the future. For education which is full of uncertainties, exploratory scenarios will usually be more appropriate. These are created in order to understand just how different the future may become and what may drive these changes. Exploratory scenarios should be: *plausible* (logical, consistent and believable), *relevant* (highlight key challenges and dynamics of the future), *divergent* (differ from one another in strategically significant ways) and *challenging* (challenge fundamental beliefs and assumptions).

Much of the scenario content is often created by a group of people (a scenario group), guided and facilitated by a scenario team that has performed the preparatory work of the first two phases described above. The scenario group may consist of representatives from the customer and/or experts appointed by the customer in combination with the scenario team. In this phase, the task of the team is to use the knowledge generated in the first two phases as input to the development of the scenarios. The scenario creation process itself will take varying time to complete, depending on the complexity of the issues involved and the goals to be met, and will often move through the following phases:

- Identification of drivers and trends.

- Consolidation of trends.
- Prioritisation of trends.
- Identification of scenario axes.
- Actor analysis.

## *Identification of drivers and trends*

Although the scenario team may already have identified a wide range of drivers and trends in their preparation, it may well be important for the scenario group to get the opportunity to brainstorm on drivers and trends. This can identify the areas and possible trends that were not well covered in the second phase.

---

**Box 6.1. Techniques for "out of the box thinking"**

- Drawing on the *stream of consciousness* concept from literature, one tool is to ask a participant to do a stream of consciousness on a concept or picture. While the participant is doing his or her stream of consciousness, the other participants are inspired to come with new drivers and trends which they write down.

- Ask one or more of the participants to use *metaphors* to describe the dynamics and drivers of change. An example could be to describe an organisational unit and the potential developments of its external relations as if it were a Savannah in Africa – who are the lions, who are the untouchable elephants, is there a waterhole and, if so, is it full of crocodiles? The other participants may then be inspired by the internal logic of the Savannah system to see new trends and drivers of change in the subject domain.

- Work with *forced pairs* in which two categories of different concepts both related to the subject are prepared by the scenario team. For example: if the subject is the school of the future, one category could be concepts of possible breakthrough technologies and the other category concepts of traditional learning and social activities in the school. Participants take turns drawing a concept from each category and will then have to create a story-line based on the pair. While the storyline is being developed, the other participants may write down new drivers inspired by the forced pairs.

---

To get participants to think "out of the box" is a difficult task. A brainstorming session therefore typically consists of two parts. In the first, everybody is asked to write on post-its all the drivers and trends influencing the subject which are then displayed for all to see. When the participants have seen all the post-its, they may then add a few if inspired by the contributions of the other participants. This first part will typically reproduce many of the ideas generated by the scenario team through the convergent methodologies. Therefore, different tools are applied in the second part to facilitate "out of the box thinking" and stimulate participants to come up with trends not previously thought of (see Box 6.1).

## Consolidation of trends

When the brainstorming phase is finished, the participants will typically have produced between 50 and 200 post-its with description of drivers, many of which will be the same or be very closely related to each other. In order to reduce the degree of complication, the drivers and trends should therefore be consolidated into some generic categories. There may be anywhere between 10 to 30 generic categories which are then be used in the future work.

## Prioritisation of trends

The aim of this phase is to gain some perspective on the relationship between the drivers and identify those which seem most suitable and interesting to form the back-bone of the scenarios. Different open and closed voting systems may be used to determine the most important factors.

*Cross impact analysis* for example, is a useful tool to illuminate the relationships between the different drivers and trends identified in the consolidation phase of the scenario workshop. Each driver's influence on the other drivers is valued on a scale from 1-10 (10 meaning strong impact). The numeric values entered may then be used in different ways. One way is to take the three highest scoring factors as the most important since they have the strongest impact on the other factors. Another way is to determine as the most important factors those which influence the largest number of the other factors which score more than 6 points. In other words, the calculations may be made in different ways as long as it is done in a consistent manner which allows the comparison of the trends and drivers and identifies the most "important" ones, according to different specifications of what this means.

A *rabbit race* is a faster but less analytical tool. Each factor is written on a post-it note and displayed on a "race track" consisting of a starting line, a finish line and 7 to 10 steps in between. In a number of rounds each participant takes turns moving a factor 1 step closer to the goal line. Each round, a number of post-its move closer to the finish line, as the participants physically move the post-it of their choice. When a certain number (say, 2-4) have reached the goal line, the exercise is stopped with the main factors thereby identified.

Although it is intuitively appealing to make the strongest drivers the backbone of a scenario, a *priority matrix* shows other considerations and approaches (see Table 6.1). For example, there may be great uncertainties with some drivers, while others are much more certain (demographic developments are a good example of the latter). Another issue is the organisation's opportunity to influence or act on a given driver. As a rule of thumb, the most "interesting" drivers to work with in a scenario context are those positioned in the "strategic uncertainties" quadrant.

**Table 6.1. Priority matrix: types of drives by degrees of uncertainty and influence**

|  | Low degree of influence | High degree of influence |
|---|---|---|
| High uncertainty | Wildcards | Strategic uncertainties |
| Low uncertainty | Trends | Given factors |

*Source*: Author.

## *Identification of the scenario structure*

The challenge in this phase is to manage the complexity of the many drivers in a way that will allow the team to create a range of internally consistent scenarios. There are many ways to make a scenario structure of which two of the most popular are presented below.

A structure is created by selecting two of the most important drivers identified in the previous phase to create a matrix of four different scenarios. The advantage of this method is that it is a relatively simple way to create scenarios, without too many drivers with too many different values. The rest of the identified drivers are then expanded within the logic of the four different scenarios to see how they would play out. This can be excellent for developing in scenarios through participatory methods. The disadvantage is primarily in the uncertainties of the two selected drivers that are played out, which may lead to the "scenario space" being too confined (Box 6.2).

> **Box 6.2. Example of a matrix with four scenarios**
>
> An example of a matrix with four scenarios could be the following on "The School in Europe in 2015". The driver "parents' social values in relation to their children's education" is considered to be the most important driver of change. The two different values of this driver are: a "my kids first" culture and a "social responsibility" culture. The other important driver is "national governments' investments schemes in schooling", and the values of this are "visionary" and "conservative".
>
> |  | Conservative investment | Visionary investment |
> | --- | --- | --- |
> | **Social responsibility** | More burdens to the communities | Shared faith and visions for all |
> | **My kids first** | Private schools rule | The choice is yours |

A multiple-driver scenario approach increases the level of complexity of the work, but may result in scenarios that are closer to reality. In principle, any number of drivers greater than 4 may be used in this method. Values are identified for each driver in the same manner as in the previous method. This means that if nine drivers have been identified, then $2^9$ scenarios may be developed. Clearly this number of scenarios is impractical, so the challenge is to identify the three to four scenarios that best fill the "scenarios space". The advantage of this method is that it allows practitioners to develop complex yet consistent scenarios which lend themselves to work on possible implications of the different scenarios. The disadvantage of this approach is the difficulty of managing the decision on which scenarios to choose, since choosing four scenarios out of so many is not an obvious matter.

## *Actor analysis*

The aim of this form of analysis is to enrich the focus on drivers and trends with one on actors. Who are the most important actors in the scenarios and how may they be expected to act in the scenarios? These questions are important if the scenarios are to be plausible and usable tools for identifying the implications of different possible futures. Identifying the actors can be done using the same methods as to identify trends. Once a range of actors has been identified, their importance should be evaluated; again this may use some of the same methods as with the drivers.

## Using the scenarios

The result of the previous phases is a set of snap-shot scenarios – "snap-shots" because there may be little accompanying information on the events leading to the situations they depict. When the scenarios are to be used for decision making and problem solving, more work may usefully be dedicated to understand how they came into being. The main approach to this is *back-casting,* where the story of the scenario is told backwards from the future "snap-shot" back to the present. A method for back-casting is to describe "headlines", retracing the situation in the scenario back to the present year by year, asking questions like: we now know what the future will be but what would the situation one year earlier have had to have been for this to be realistic?

Once a richer scenario structure has been developed, it may be used for different kinds of strategic analysis and/or policy formulation. Scenarios are tools for a structured conversation and analysis of the future, and the temptation should be resisted of picking the most preferred and/or likely scenario to analyse how it may be realised. Instead, the goal should be to understand the dynamics of change and use the insights generated to identify initiatives that may do well under all the scenarios options and under most circumstances.

The scenario method may be used in policy context in different ways ranging from the exploration of different issues to being aides to explicit decision-making: most uses of scenarios lie somewhere on the spectrum from, on the one side, exploration to, on the other, supporting the decision-making process. Here, three main uses of scenarios are discussed, as well as their implications for design.

### *Developing shared knowledge of the environment*

The exploratory aspects of scenario development can prove to be invaluable for policy and administration. Often, there are deeply rooted and culturally-based assumptions about the nature of the environment of the administrative unit and its policy area. Working with scenarios may help the participants to challenge and re-conceptualise their understanding of the administrative environment and the dynamics and trends that shape it. The major outcome of using scenarios may indeed be in challenging existing understandings. This may call for a rapid and uncumbersome project design, if the main objective is to sharpen understanding of the policy, organisation or the sector's environment instead of using this in problem-solving activity.

If this is the case, relatively few resources are used in phase two; the desk research conducted in phase one can be complemented with some interviews with key personnel to ensure that a correct understanding of the subject matter has been formed. Phase three can also be designed with minimal resources. Trends and drivers may be identified through the metaphor tool and prioritised in a rapid, simple manner, perhaps via the "rabbit race". Finally, the scenarios can be developed with the "two by two matrix", allowing the participants themselves to create the scenarios relatively quickly. The actual work developing the scenarios may last no longer than a full-day workshop. In phase four, the results of the previous phases are reported and a list of recommendations and/or activities related to the subject may be formulated.

## *Using scenarios to strengthen public discourse*

There may be a political interest in initiating or strengthening a public discourse, including as many stakeholders as possible, and again scenarios may prove useful to this end. Different scenarios may help to frame the issues and hence may be a way to guide public discourse. Stakeholders may be included at an early phase of the process, thereby taking ownership of it at an early stage as well as the dissemination of results. This calls for a more robust and resource-intensive process design, since a greater number of information sources and stakeholders must be involved and there are greater demands on the scenarios to be consistent and precise if they are to be so used publicly.

This means in the first phase that more attention needs to be paid to mapping the subject area, especially stakeholders' relationships to the subject. In phase two, stakeholders should be involved, perhaps via focus groups, conferences, and/or workshops, and the team needs to ensure the adequate documentation of the stakeholders' input. In phase three, a group of the major stakeholders and experts on the subject would usually develop the scenarios so as to ensure the quality of the process and the reflection of the stakeholders' inputs. Since the trends should be evaluated thoroughly, cross-impact analysis is a good tool to identify the key trends. To be a useful tool for debate, the scenarios should not be too complex, and often the "two by two matrix" is appropriate.

To generate debate, workshops or focus groups with representatives from the dominant stakeholders can usefully present and discuss the major conclusions and questions from the study. Using the feedback from these sessions, the final reports can be fine-tuned and a communications strategy can be developed. The communications strategy will depend on the subject, but may usefully include interactive and participatory activities such as conferences or discussion forums on the Internet if the public discourse is to be strengthened.

## *Using scenarios for decision support*

A third widespread use of scenarios in a policy context is to support decisions on complex issues with long-term implications. This use requires very well-researched and robust scenarios, normally with a large amount of quantifiable data.

In phase two, interviews with key personnel and focus groups can be devoted to broadening the understanding of the subject and possible trade-offs among the different decisions to be taken. In phase three, it is important that the design group needs to be clear as to how uncertain are the different drivers and how these drivers may themselves be influenced, as strategic decisions will be taken on the basis of the different scenarios. The priority matrix may well be used to identify the most important drivers, but if resources permit, a cross-impact analysis may be very useful as well. Since the scenarios are to be used as an analytical tool, the multiple-driver approach will often be the most appropriate.

Once the scenarios have been created they are put into action. They can be "back-cast" in order to understand plausible lines of development leading to each one. Different tools can be used for the assessment of how decisions may play out in the different scenarios. If the decisions are closely related to an organisation, a "Strengths, Weaknesses, Opportunities and Threats analysis" (SWOT) may be conducted in order to assess the implications of the different scenarios for the organisation. Based on these inputs, a more informed decision can then be taken. Once it is taken, a set of criteria should be developed to measure the key drivers and trends identified in the scenarios. This will allow the team and administrative unit to monitor future progress towards the scenarios. In the case of major discrepancies between scenarios and reality, the decisions and pathways need to be reviewed.

## Conclusions – enhancing success in using scenarios

It is useful to consider in conclusion a number of factors that will increase the success of using the scenario method. The dynamics of bureaucracy tend to make administrative personnel (and politicians) risk-averse. Much of the policy and administrative discourse is tied into "objective" macro economic discourses and models which can be related to economic rules, which also has the effect of taking responsibility beyond the individual employee. This poses two challenges for working with scenarios in a policy context. First, scenarios are often considered to be anything but objective but they can be *just as fact-based as reasoning within a macro economic discourse*. It helps to bring this to the fore. Second, habits and conservatism may be hard to overcome and there is an element of risk involved in engaging in a totally new method where the results may be hard to predict. For this reason, it is important that *all scenario procedures be made clear* for everybody.

*Creating ownership* is needed for the scenario process to become successful. Leadership of the organisation or unit involved must support it for it to succeed as often it differs from the regular ways of doing business and hence can create anxiety: clear supportive statements from management may help to alleviate this. Participants from all levels must engage wholeheartedly throughout the entire process in order to develop robust and thought-provoking scenarios.

When deciding which stakeholders and experts to include in the process the team responsible should *try to think as broadly and inclusively as possible*. It is often beneficial if those involved are diverse so as to stimulate a certain creative tension throughout the process. If not all important actors can be directly involved, extra expert committees or advisory groups can be created and given an opportunity to contribute.

Scenario development may involve anxiety and frustration. The initial uncertainties and openness of the process mean that participants may find it difficult to see how it will lead to sound and consistent results. Therefore the scenario team must do its best to describe the logic behind the design and every phase in it to *minimise the anxiety of participants and stakeholders*.

A well-designed future study must *balance divergent and convergent thinking*. Convergent thinking is essentially about traditional problem solving while divergent thinking is a skill broadly related to the creative elaboration of ideas prompted by a stimulus. These two ways of thinking need to be combined in order to facilitate a process that is exploratory and creative, yet factually-based with explicit assumptions.

So, notwithstanding that scenarios should be made fit for purpose, there are some general success factors that offer guiding principles for working with scenarios.

# *References*

Godet, M. and F. Roubelat (1996), "Creating the Future, The Use and Misuse of Scenarios", *Long Range Planning*, Vol. 29, No. 2, pp. 164-171.

van der Heijden, K. (1996), *Scenarios, the Art of Strategic Conversation*, Wiley, Chichester.

Loveridge, D. (1999), "Foresight and Delphi Processes as Information Sources for Scenario Planning. Ideas in Progress", Paper Number 11, PREST University of Manchester.

Mercer, D. (1997), "Robust Strategies in a Day", *Management and Decision*, Vol. 35, pp. 129-223.

Schwartz, P. (1984/1997), *The Art of the Long View*, John Wiley and Sons.

van Wyk, R. (1997), "Strategic Technology Scanning", *Technology Forecasting and Social Change*, Vol. 55, pp. 21-38.

# Part Two

# Futures Thinking in Action

# Chapter 7
# England: using scenarios to build capacity for leadership[1]

*The English FutureSight initiative was built through a multi-partnership approach to develop practical applications of futures thinking which school leaders could use to shape, not just guess at, the future. FutureSight is a tool for school leaders which makes more explicit the values and goals that drive decisions, thereby engaging the school's stakeholders in creating the future together. The chapter describes both the tool itself and how it was developed and used. The four-module cycle involves addressing key trends, understanding alternative futures these might lead to, identifying preferred futures for schools, and comparing the preferred and current arrangements.*

## Systems and policy context

The United Kingdom has a devolved national education system, linked to strong, centrally directed target-setting. Education policy in England in the 1990s was characterised by a sustained period of school improvement, closely allied to public accountability measures. This central drive for improvement led to the emergence of data-rich schools and centrally directed initiatives around teaching and learning, such as the national literacy and numeracy strategies.

The early years of the 21st century have brought a sharper focus, with the improvement movement seeking to explore more radical thinking. Despite significant gains, national and international analyses of student outcomes suggest that education in England is still not serving all pupils well – particularly in the secondary sector. The message seems clear: if England continues to do what it has always done, it would get what it has

---

[1] Report written by Jane Creasy and Sarah Harris, National College for School Leadership (NCSL).

always got. Decision makers are therefore moving away from "one-size-fits-all" solutions to give schools more space and authority and themselves seeking ways of allowing this to happen without compromising the standards agenda – still a key policy imperative. Different schools have different challenges and the goal was to understand what policy contexts would enable England to redesign learning so that the needs of the entire population can be met.

## Goals of initiatives

The FutureSight Toolkit grew out of work undertaken by the National College for School Leadership (NCSL) and its partners, the Innovation Unit at the Department for Education and Skills (DfES) and the think-tank Demos, as part of the international OECD "Schooling for Tomorrow" project (*www.ncsl.org.uk/research/research_activities/randd-future-index.cfm*). The purpose of the work was to develop practical applications of the ideas around futures thinking which school leaders could use to do more than guess at the future. In parallel with projects in the Netherlands, Canada and New Zealand, the work has contributed to the international "toolbox" of futures approaches.

The project was launched in England in 2002 and offered the potential for policy makers and educational leaders to step outside the intractable problems of the present, at school and system level, to see the future of learning in new, challenging and exciting ways. FutureSight uses the concepts and techniques of futures thinking to explore the nature of the choices we face. As we are creating the future today, by the decisions we take now, FutureSight is a way to reveal the expectations and values that shape our current decisions and to begin imagining new options for creating our preferred future. It is a tool for school leaders who want to make the values and goals that drive decisions more explicit, thereby engaging the school's stakeholders in creating the future together. It has the potential to make an impact on strategic thinking both in schools and more widely across the education system. The FutureSight tool challenges school leaders to look over the horizon, to understand the direction in which the system is travelling, articulate a desired future, consider the relationship between that preferred future and the current reality, and, along the way, draw out some of the inconsistencies and discontinuities of policy and practice.

The approach has been to focus on school leaders and the development of processes to make use of the Futuesight material as a vehicle for leadership learning. The focus on school leaders as agents of system change and improvement has been a prevailing political and educational theme for some years. Beyond the responsibility for an individual school, there is increasing recognition of the principal's contribution to system development. In recognising the difficulty and complexity of engaging in sustainable system-wide change, Michael Fullan's view of the central importance of integration between the levels of the system particularly resonates with the FutureSight materials; to that extent, FutureSight seeks to equip key agents of change, namely school leaders working collaboratively, to contribute to both policy formulation and enactment and to lead our map-making journey towards a preferred future.

## Process design

The FutureSight Toolkit was developed through an iterative process, involving a sequence of seminars. A conceptual framework and shared vocabulary emerged to help group participants understand the relationship between the reality of the current context and the worlds described in the scenarios. Participants led the team into ways of exploring the scenarios, of walking around in these imagined futures and, finally, of designing tools to enable us to use the scenarios more analytically. In reaching this point, we have tried, tested, abandoned, and adapted tools and processes.

The first seminar, at the end of 2002, brought together leaders, chief executives and senior officers from national training and development organisations, alongside interested head teachers. Six months later a group of school leaders from schools facing challenging circumstances[2] worked through the developing toolkit. These tools were then adapted for a seminar with older secondary students through an event hosted by the University of the First Age, a Birmingham-based charity promoting innovative learning with young people. School leaders from the Innovation Unit's Leading Edge Partnership schools[3] also met to experience the seminars and contribute further. Such a process has continued with other school and local authority groups since publication. In May 2004, we held a seminar to enable senior policy makers to consider the implications and potential of this work.

From the workshops, a tangible product, the FutureSight Toolkit was developed. It is a full set of materials for a facilitator and ten participants over a 24-hour seminar. Using the OECD trends and scenarios as source material, the learning framework, tools and processes are designed to have relevance for, and be used in, a range of different contexts.

---

[2] Schools, often in high poverty communities, deemed as facing circumstances which make the achievement of central performance standards particularly challenging.

[3] Secondary schools with a record of success, as measured by current accountability criteria, and given funding to work in partnership with other schools.

## Scenario content

### *England's FutureSight Toolkit*

In the FutureSight programme, participants are encouraged to consider how children of 2020 will want to learn, and how schools will need to change to meet those needs. The FutureSight process expects participants to draw on their tacit knowledge and experience which is then combined with the trends and scenarios of the OECD "Schooling for Tomorrow" project. The various activities enable participants to uncover the values and assumptions that influence their thinking, and to travel from current reality to preferred futures.

The four modules are, however, designed for sequential use and the progression is explicit. This is because the scenarios have been found to have greater authority when they build on an appreciation of the powerful trends which shape them. In turn, discussion of preferred futures has greater authenticity when this follows the experience of imagining what life would be like in, or "walking around", the different scenarios which seem distant from our own experience.

The four modules are as follows:

1. A stone rolling

- Introduction to process, key ideas and vocabulary.
- Exploring the trends and checking them against today's reality.
- Rolling them forward to 2020.

2. Making it real

- Introduction to scenarios.
- Tools to help experience the scenarios from the perspective of pupils, parents and educators and other stakeholders.

3. Towards a preferred future

- Tools to analyse desirable and undesirable aspects of scenarios and reach consensus over a shared, preferred future.

4. Re-engaging with the present

- Processes and tools to reflect on our current direction of travel and the ways in which we might influence both direction and speed of travel.

The first module, "a stone rolling", is designed to enable participants to engage with what is already known about trends in wider society that will affect the future of schools. The first step is simply to discuss the trends at a general level. Participants are subsequently asked to share their own experiences and perceptions relating to these trends; to describe how they are manifest in different schools; to think about which are having most impact; and to suggest other trends which they see as having an impact in their context.

The second module "making it real" is based on OECD's six schooling scenarios. These scenarios describe how the same trends discussed earlier could combine to produce different futures. A "hot-seating" exercise drawn from drama provides opportunities for participants to work in groups of three, with each person assuming the role of a student, or a parent/carer, or an adult professional within the context of one of the six scenarios. Having considered what their experience of the given scenario might be like, they then respond, in role, to questions from the rest of the wider group. The purpose of this activity is to enable participants to make sense of and internalise the different scenarios without making judgements about their desirability. Key ground rules are an agreement to resist talking about the present or the desirability/probability of the scenarios and to accept the challenge of the scenario by careful avoidance of stereotypes.

In the third module, "towards a preferred future", participants co-construct a "preferred future" based on their own beliefs and values. They engage in scenario building themselves, using the OECD content as a starting point but encouraged to combine it in new ways in the form of a board game and to write their own content. This module provides a key opportunity to challenge assumptions and to surface values. It also plays a valuable role in developing agreed and explicit meanings, a process which can otherwise be overlooked, as assumptions are made about implicit understanding.

The fourth module, "re-engaging with the present", is designed to enable participants to reflect on the differences between their current reality and their preferred futures and to identify the barriers and enablers that will affect their future trajectory. The mixture of board game and reflective tasks serves to strengthen both creative responses and ensure that they relate to existing circumstances and trends. This learning can then be used to inform strategic thinking as participants develop their schools or organisations.

## Scenario usage

The FutureSight Toolkit was officially launched in September 2004 to an audience of over 120 school leaders, local authority officials and colleagues from networked learning communities. The publication of the materials coincided with the launch and by mid-2005 a further print run had been ordered. The NCSL has made the toolkit available to order on its website and is also running facilitation workshops on a regional level to train for its use, as well as leading seminars of groups wanting to experience the process themselves. These have been taken up by a number of local education authorities, frequently those engaged with policy initiatives with long-term implications. At the time of writing, more than 700 school leaders, LEA officers/advisers, policy makers and international participants have been involved in the FutureSight activity since the project began. Given that a good number of these people are in a position to lead workshops with others, using the FutureSight pack, the potential reach is many times this figure.

A number of participants has explained how the FutureSight process has helped them alter their analytical approaches to cope with the ambiguity of a future full of different possibilities. In dealing with the process of policy formulation, rather than just implementation, many felt they were able to release creative energies to produce new and exciting ideas .One secondary school principal particularly remembers the "hot-seating" technique, a role play in which delegates were questioned by their colleagues:

*"It made you think outside the box, widening your experience and perception of what the future could hold. Since then, it has helped me think more broadly and at the possibility of a number of solutions, whereas in the past it has been easier to look along a single tried and trusted line."*

Another senior school head from the East of England found the training invaluable in planning for the future of his own school, which is about to undergo a major facility upgrade:

*"Applying the FutureSight process to our own situation enabled us to shape a vision of where we wanted to go and build according to the concept of an extended school."*

*"Without this sort of thinking we might have got bogged down by existing realities, and could well have ended up simply redesigning a school which was created 30 or 40 years ago."*

*"FutureSight helped us feel more secure about changing things and being radical."*

A London primary head has also been using her FutureSight experience to good effect:

*"It has helped us to be more positive about challenging existing practice and thinking about new solutions to existing and future problems."*

*"Through discussion, we discovered that tracking down and arranging resources was wasting large amounts of teacher's time. From September we are appointing a support assistant with responsibility for organising, arranging and collecting resources for the whole school."*

*"Long term, we are beginning to address issues such as class size, deployment of teaching and specialist support staff, flexible contracts both in terms of hours in a day and weeks in a year."*

*"It is all about challenging what you do – to see if you can do it better."*

This principal has also become an active FutureSight facilitator for other events, as have a number of others who were involved in the developmental seminars.

## Outcomes

In summary, the findings from the experience of working with the materials and the evaluation and other feedback, suggest that the following concepts are key areas which are developed:

- *Living with ambiguity* – challenging the conventional predisposition to treat problems in a linear way and to seek answers.

- *Inhabiting the future* – finding ways of interrogating thinking about possible futures in ways which make them real. A "hot-seating" tool was developed to enable participants to explore a future scenario and share how it feels from a range of different perspectives. Ground rules were developed to challenge people to live in the future and to adopt naïve approaches to questioning through the idea of a "veil of ignorance".

- *Challenging of assumptions* – however open-minded we may regard ourselves, we all have ideas about what the future might be like, often based on our prejudices and preferences. The FutureSight process encourages people to challenge these assumptions and try looking at possible futures in new ways.

- *Making values explicit* – the processes involved, particularly in the third module, where participants examine a preferred future, allow for exploration of values and offer a strong message about the importance of making values explicit when bringing stakeholders together for futures thinking. *"The discussion regarding the semantics of the cards was useful for exposing values – it was a way of getting to the heart of the issue."*

The evaluation responses from those involved in the FutureSight process since publication have been overwhelmingly positive, though it is too early to judge the depth of the impact on strategic activity. We do know, however, that participants register significantly profound learning outcomes from the process:

- *Collaborative learning* – the residential nature of the seminar brings an intensity to the collaborative work which appears to deepen the process by enabling people to move from their "default" position in thinking about tackling future issues. This is particularly true when the seminar participants are not part of an existing team. The experience is further enhanced by the use of a core group of facilitators who have first experienced the process and then work with others through the materials/seminar.

- *Conceptual framework and language* – one of the key areas of learning for participants has been the development of specific language and concepts for talking about futures and thereby deepening futures thinking. This specific language/concept development seems key to releasing imaginations to deal with the ambiguity and possibility mentioned above. *"I found this really useful. The 'veil of ignorance' concept was really effective."*

- *Big–picture thinking* – the fact that the scenarios deal with policy-level ideas raises school leaders' sights beyond the everyday and beyond preoccupations with implementation, to provide space for creating a bigger picture within which they can make sense of their own work. *"It is so good to be allowed to think for ourselves, rather than being told what to think and do."*

## Further outcomes

Another outcome has been the further developmental work undertaken by the Innovation Unit, based on the FutureSight materials and processes. In the light of the policy agenda on personalisation, the unit gathered 30 successful and forward–looking heads together who could work with adapted materials to develop a "visualisation" process around personalisation, and then act as advocates and facilitators for others. Working with a design company, with Demos, and with NCSL, a seminar process was developed which drew on much of the original FutureSight seminar (including the trends, scenarios and "hot-seating") and then made use of specially-commissioned pictures and words to stimulate thinking about what a personalised future might look like. This pack has since been produced and marketed, and some regional sessions have taken place. Although smaller than FutureSight, it offers an example of the same approach to a specific policy issue.

Other indicators come from the level of Local Education Authority (LEA) interest and the number of sessions being requested for LEA groups of head teachers. Given developments like Every Child Matters and Building Schools for the Future, as well as personalization,[4] local authorities and groups of schools are seeking ways of addressing big issues about future shape of provision; FutureSight offers a powerful tool to support such thinking.

The use of the materials with students has also been an outcome from the seminar work. In addition to individual schools developing sessions on the basis of their FutureSight experience, a separate set of student materials has been developed within the Community Leadership programme, in partnership with the University of the First Age.

Respondents have reported with some feeling on the potential value of the process for enhancing the policy-practice debate, with strong indication that the materials provide a scaffold and discipline which challenges preconceived notions and ways of working. They spark imaginative responses to trends which have been derived from rigorous analysis and legitimise the exploration and interrogation of alternative viewpoints through the use of "naïve" questions.

## Implications for policy makers

Given the significant change being enacted in the English system at present, and the opportunities being presented by policy emphasis on, for

---

[4] Further information on these policy issues can be found at:
Personalisation: *www.standards.dfes.gov.uk/personalisedlearning/*;
*www.standards.dfes.gov.uk/innovation-unit/*;
Workforce remodelling: *www.remodelling.org/*
Inclusion and wellbeing: *www.everychildmatters.gov.uk/*
New buildings: *www.number-10.gov.uk/output/Page5801.asp*

example, personalisation, workforce remodelling, inclusion and wellbeing for all children, and the physical improvement and development of school buildings, there is a place for those involved in policy to employ a set of tools which help both to discipline and release futures thinking.

One significant issue which is worth addressing here, however, is "Who should be involved in such policy-related thinking?". At the Toronto "Schooling for Tomorrow" Forum, June 2004, Jay Ogilvy suggested that educational change has frequently foundered because it has addressed "bits" of the system, whereas it is the system itself that needs to change. The implication, therefore, is that to engage in futures thinking at system level, it is necessary to involve a range of different perspectives – to get a full cross-section of views around the table. This view receives some support from Michael Fullan (2004) in *Leadership and Sustainability: System Thinkers in Action*. He suggests that if a system is striving for both "high equity and excellence" then policy and practice have to focus on system improvement. He explores the relationship between individual leadership and system transformation and argues that a dynamic relationship between the two is essential. The FutureSight Toolkit may offer a vehicle for engaging a range of voices amongst leaders and policy makers, to enable thinking on a number of strategic issues and involve the vertical and lateral connections that Fullan suggests are vital for sustainable change.

# *Reference*

Fullan, M. (2004), *Leadership and Sustainability: System Thinkers in Action*, Sage Publications, Corwin Press, USA.

# Chapter 8
# The Netherlands: futures thinking in innovation, school organisation and leadership development

> *The Dutch government's steering philosophy in education has combined decentralisation and more autonomy for schools, with a greater influence of the stakeholders – parents, students and the local community. Innovation means that schools have the ability to organise their classroom teaching differently, not following a new "grand design" for teaching. The first Dutch initiative featured in this chapter has focused on capacity building for visionary leadership through the events organised by the Dutch Principals Academy on future thinking for school leaders. The second project focuses on one example of a radical innovation in schooling – Slash/21 – which is a school "redesigned" by KPC, a consulting group working in education and partly financed by government.*

## Introduction

The Netherlands has participated in the OECD "Schooling for Tomorrow" project as a "laboratory of change", both using the scenarios and in other activities aimed at enhancing futures thinking in education.[1] This chapter describes two projects that were carried out in the Netherlands against the background of major changes in the Dutch government's steering philosophy in education. Briefly, this new steering philosophy combined decentralisation and more autonomy for schools, with a greater influence of the stakeholders: parents, students and the local community.

---

[1] The Dutch study team for Schooling for Tomorrow were Jan Heijmans, Dutch Principals Academy, Harry Gankema, KPC Group, and Anneke Boot (Ministry of Education, Culture and Science).

One of the ideas behind the new steering philosophy has been that top-down modernisation is not effective, because it is too uniform and does not address the situation in which professionals work. The development of education is a continual process in which a school community determines, from the bottom up, what changes are preferred for their own organisation in their own environment. Innovation means that schools have the ability to organise their classroom teaching differently, not following a new "grand design" for teaching. It means innovation is shaped from and by schools. The first Dutch initiative focused on capacity building for visionary leadership; the Dutch Principals Academy ran a series of events focusing on futures thinking and visionary leadership for school leaders. The second project focuses on one example of a radical innovation in schooling – Slash/21. This is a school "redesigned" by the KPC Group, a consulting group working in education and partly financed by government. One of the consequences of the new steering philosophy is the identified need for leadership capacity at the school level. Decentralisation has meant that school leaders need to think about where they want to take their school.

## New educational governance

New educational governance is characterised by: deregulation, a limited setting of frameworks on the part of the national government, greater space given to institutions themselves, incentives for the optimum utilisation of the available space, and the need for accountability to government and society by the institutions about the choices they make and monitoring of compliance with the established frameworks. Government has established clear frameworks, like attainment targets and examination programmes, and provides incentives to work within them; it has reduced regulation in order to give schools greater room to take their own initiative and responsibility. By 2006, every school will be funded through receipt of a lump sum budget to give them greater freedom.

One of the instruments in this new steering philosophy is the development of multi-year policy plans, for each sector of education. These plans outline the general direction for a certain sector over the coming years; they provide a vision of the future for the sector in the short term (the four years of a cabinet term) and the longer term (eight to ten years). The process of developing these plans is important. The close co-operation between the ministry, school leaders, teachers, students, parents, and other public bodies in the neighbourhood of the school enhances the field's capacity for futures thinking. The aim is to develop a common vision and policy programme for each sector. The main themes vary by sector. In primary education, the main themes chosen were: education quality and innovation, teaching staff and organisation, and the social role of the school in relation to its environment. The plans were discussed in Parliament and subsequently established by government, indicating for each theme what steps will be taken in the short and long term (see Box 8.1).

> **Box 8.1. Principles of the new education system governance in the Netherlands**
>
> - The administration of the educational institution supports its teaching staff and encourages and challenges its staff to assume personal responsibility within their field of expertise.
>
> - The administration, as the competent authority, is primarily responsible for the educational institution, and thus also for the choices to be made between, sometimes conflicting, interests of various stakeholders.
>
> - The duties and responsibilities of administration and supervision must be transparent.
>
> - The involvement of pupils, participants, students and parents is safeguarded.
>
> - The involvement of the social partners – the business sector and social organisations – is safeguarded.
>
> - The organisations acting as representatives within the various education sectors will assume more responsibility.
>
> - More attention must be paid to accountability to the social environment of the educational institution; this accountability, however, can never completely replace vertical supervision by the Ministry of Education.
>
> - The supervision of the Ministry is focused at the legitimacy and quality of education and to a lesser extent governance. The Minister will be able to intervene in the event of a serious failure.
>
> - A proper balance must be found between internal supervision, horizontal accountability and the supervision of the central government.

Evaluations of this new and interactive process have shown solid and consistent progress in terms of a "renewal of relations". The relation between the demand side of schooling (parents and students) and the supply side (school leaders and teachers) has become stronger, while existing relations *e.g.* between government and representative organisations of the sector have weakened. Representative organisations are looking for new channels to exercise voice – the Parliament, mass media and specialised education media. A fundamental change in the style of policy-making and the organisation of education is taking place towards a diverse set of checks and balances at the local, school level and with government in an increasingly remote and supervisory role.

## The development of visionary school leadership

As noted, the decentralisation of decision-making in the Netherlands has not only stimulated and provided room for innovation; it has also created a greater need for leadership capacity at the local levels. The Dutch Principals Academy (DPA) is focused on just that. DPA is an independent non-governmental body for leaders in primary education. It stimulates and maintains the professional quality and expertise of management in primary education. The five main assignments of the DPA are: to develop and maintain a professional standard; to keep a register of competent leaders in primary education; to accredit and certify the programmes for professionalisation; to develop the starter qualifications of the profession; and to establish a Dutch Centre for Leadership in Schools.

During Phase 2 of the OECD "Schooling for Tomorrow" project, the DPA focused on the core competence of visionary leadership of school leaders in primary education. DPA research made it clear that having a vision is crucial for school leaders but that they rarely have their own strong vision of what good education, good schools and good leadership will be in the future. Their ideas are heavily coloured by national policy and expertise from consultants and advisors. While visionary leadership involves long-term and broad thinking, the visions of school leaders have a limited scope and are internally focused and locally oriented. DPA sought therefore to promote long-term visionary leadership by introducing futures thinking in the initial training of leaders in primary education, through school improvement projects focused on sustainable visions for daily practice in schools. It aimed to develop, try out and evaluate instruments, methods and other working materials that challenge head teachers to develop their own visions, appealing to their role as leaders of a moral enterprise and their professional responsibility to co-create desirable futures. DPA also sought to obtain images and evidence of preferred and disliked futures from different groups of school leaders.

### *Design and methodology*

The original six OECD scenarios outlined what possible school models might be in the future whereas DPA wanted leaders in primary education to create their own images. Therefore, it used the five broad societal scenarios from the Ontario "Teaching as a Profession" project as a basis, adapted to the European context and combining them with the outcomes of the pre-forward study from the Ministry of Education, Culture and Science. This resulted in the following five scenarios:

- *In a united Europe*: in this scenario, the structures and processes of education remain similar to what they are now. Government will be more effective and reliable, and sound economic policies result in steady economic growth. The education system is highly standardised with an emphasis on the quality of educational programmes as well as on accountability for quality.

- *In a downward spiral*: in this depressing, unstable future there is great unemployment and labour unrest. Regional conflicts and wars lead to large numbers of refugees and create problems for international trade. Innovation in the education system primarily focuses on efficiency and providing effective low-cost service. The education system becomes smaller and less accessible, and alternative forms of education increase.

- *For community and environmental care*: this scenario focuses on changes in communal life. Due to several environmental disasters, there is a growing and worldwide interest in the environment. Large numbers of self-providing communities develop strong local cultures and take a greater responsibility for education.

- *In a global market economy*: in this vision of the future, the scale of multi-national corporations increases quickly. The borders between corporate and national interests are blurring. Both public and private sectors acknowledge the importance of education for economic development. Lifelong learning becomes the norm.

- *In a high-tech networking society*: in this scenario technology provides the means for the complex networks within which people communicate and learn. Education is aimed at the individuals' changing preferences and interests and its main responsibility is for refining and stimulating people's desire to learn.

## *Activities*

These scenarios were used in diverse ways in different sessions all aimed at stimulating visionary thinking with school heads. To stimulate creative thinking, mixed groups of leaders in primary education were placed in the imaginary worlds of the five scenarios. Different methods were used to let them design and evaluate stories and images of future schools for

2-15-year-old children in 2030. There were three *writing sessions* with over 100 participants. Sessions were held with (deputy) heads – who were asked to write short stories as a team of educational designers to describe schools in one of the scenarios. Another writing session was organised for 20 aspiring heads in initial training to describe a school day of a 4-year-old and a 12-year-old child in 2030.

Second, there were three *walking sessions* with around 50 participants in which mixed groups (deputy heads, heads of innovative schools), walked in different environments like a museum of modern art, a zoo, a history museum and a space centre, in order to get impressions and experiences of learning in the future. They made pictures for a powerpoint presentation on five school design dimensions (see Box 8.2), and the presentations were then used to discuss possible futures.

---

**Box 8.2. Five school dimensions**

To create images of possible future schools in the scenarios and to be able to analyse results in a systematic way a framework with five school design dimensions was used:

- Why should one learn? – expectations from education in the future.

- What does one have to learn? – contents and curricula in the future.

- Where and how can one learn? – learning environments and resources in the future.

- How can learning be organised? – leadership and governance in future education.

- How can learning be supported in the future? – the role of parents, local community and society.

---

Third, an *information processing session* with a mixed group of around 20 aspiring superintendents in their initial training phase took place in a computer facility with Internet access. The intention was to get impressions and experiences of learning in the future on the Internet and make a powerpoint presentation on the five school design dimensions for presentation and the means to discuss possible futures.

Fourth, two *evaluation sessions* were held each with similar numbers to the previous session. The first was with head teachers of a large federation of schools, who had just put together their policy strategy, in order to assess those plans against the five scenarios and to experience how "future proof" they are. The second brought together head teachers of schools of different denominations, working closely together in an educational region, to discuss what shared opinions they had on preferred or disliked futures.

## *Results*

While there has been no formal evaluation of the initiative; feedback suggests that many school leaders have used the materials and their experience in the session to create a vision for their own school. Beyond building leadership capacity, the sessions give us some raw material to shed light on ideas about futures for education.

The "united Europe" scenario has led to the realisation that knowledge of languages and different cultures is becoming more important. At the same time the growing importance of regions within Europe points towards the need to strengthen the ties with the local community. Reactions to the "downward spiral" scenario have shown how difficult handling major change will be for the educational system, but it has also led to the realisation that schools are havens of safety and would play a key role in handling the fear and stress engendered by this future. The "community and environmental care" scenario has led to the suggestion that the boundaries between school and environment are blurring, that learning takes place both inside and outside the school, and that it is important to strengthen the relation between school, society and family. The "global market" scenario has led to the realisation that lifelong learning requires the building of attitudes supportive of it in primary education. Responses to the "high-tech networking society" have resulted in the realisation that society will be too complex for any single actor – whether government, companies or another – to guide an individual throughout life.

The whole exercise has also led to a number of core questions to be explored in the future. Who "owns" education? What is the role of politics, ideology and the professional? How to create variety without this leading to segmentation? How to strike a balance between the demand and supply of education – what do children want to learn and what must they learn? Free will of the individual vs. the uniformity of regulating processes? Educating world citizens and cherishing the local community?

## Slash/21: a re-engineered school model

The new governance philosophy of clear but limited government frameworks, in combination with institutions that must account for their results, produces considerable room for innovation from below. There are, however, a number of factors which have coincided and made the Dutch education system more innovative. The first factor is related to governance changes, whereby the new external orientation brought into the system by the greater influence of stakeholders has encouraged innovations. Also, many teachers have come to understand that the transfer of pre-defined knowledge (*i.e.* teaching) is very different from making the individual learning process relevant (*i.e.* learning). There has been, in a time of economic growth, an intense exchange with innovative initiatives in countries like Canada, Sweden, Finland and especially the work of Arthur Andersen in the Alameda school in San Francisco. Finally, representatives from national industries had an increasing influence on curricula; they promoted the idea that there should be less emphasis on formal knowledge and more on a broad range of competencies.

Slash/21 is one of the first examples of this generation of innovation in schooling and has had a substantial influence on innovations that followed. It was strongly supported by the Minister, and parents and pupils where enthusiastic. Slash/21 not only stood for a new learning approach but also for a new way of organising learning processes at the micro-, meso- and macro-levels and for new definitions of staff functions within a school. It became accepted that others worked with students, not only teachers, and that a school could operate without timetables or subject-based curricula.

The greater openness to educational innovation notwithstanding, the developers of Slash/21 perceived the school system as lagging behind fundamental changes in society. They point to substantial social changes like for example the rise of ICT that has changed the world since the 1980s while schools, the obvious institutions to deal with information and communication, are still struggling to identify what significance ICT has for education.

## *The vision behind Slash/21*

Slash/21 rests on a particular vision of the future. This vision hinges on two core concepts: the rise of the knowledge society and increasing individualisation. The *knowledge society* means that people will need the ability to apply their knowledge quickly. When new technology is introduced, those who benefit most are not those who enrol in the first available course (lifelong learning) but those who already have enough tacit knowledge to incorporate new technology into their existing knowledge set. The belief behind Slash/21 is that the knowledge society does not so much call for people who can learn quickly and throughout their lives, but more who have received basic concepts that last a lifetime. *Individualisation* means that the highly standardised nature of traditional schooling, in terms of standardised contents, levels, location and time of instruction, no longer fits with the individualised nature of children. This results in high drop-out rates, by those who fail because of school specific norms which they will never have to comply with in life outside and after school.

On this analysis, the developers envisaged Slash/21 as a service organisation for students in need of skills to operate in the society of the future. Students are treated as consumers and knowledge as something that belongs to these consumers and therefore has to be personalised. There is an emphasis on blended and informal learning and the whole world is viewed as a resource for learning. Learning is seen as something which cannot be planned in rigid time schedules and knowledge as something which cannot be defined within subject-matter boundaries. Importantly, knowledge, skills and attitudes are not derived from central curriculum goals developed from inside the system but from crucial learning moments that people have to go through on their way towards and within the world of work. In other words, the Slash/21 model sees effective learning as depending on the ability to make connections. Learning combines subjects from different disciplines and aims to create insight in the bigger picture. Energy, for example, is such a key concept: to understand it, it is important to use insights from chemistry, physics and biology and Slash/21 presents those insights in an overall setting and not separated into different subjects. Slash/21 also follows the principles of intensive language teaching: in a twelve-week period, the students work intensively in four, three-hour periods a week on one modern language. From Day One, they are motivated to speak in a foreign language, encouraged by an English, French or German native speaker who stimulates, interests and corrects the learners whenever necessary.

Slash/21 has tutors instead of teachers, assisting and stimulating students if and when necessary. For a number of reasons, tutors have more time to spend with the students. First, the teaching system is flexible and tutors are complementary to one another. Second, teaching assistants take over certain tasks and responsibilities from the tutor which traditionally the teachers would do themselves. Third, the use of an electronic learning environment provides tutors with more time and they have the opportunity to completely focus on their key roles as coach, guide, companion and supporter. Together, tutors and teaching assistants form a team guided by a team leader. They are responsible for the education of a group of students for three years, thereby encouraging a close bond between students and staff. Students too are encouraged to form groups, for group assignments are central at the Slash/21 model. Within these groups, they learn from each other and feel free to expose their opinions and emotions. There are no classes in Slash/21, just "home groups" of about 50 students. Three "home groups" of three subsequent course years are combined to one "learning community" under the supervision of a staff team. The members of the "home group" quickly know one another; therefore it is easy to split them into small and changing groups to carry out work projects. In order to give course-like tuition, "home groups" from several "learning communities" will be joined together from time to time.

For this type of education, where the pupils are expected to work in smaller or larger groups, a new type of school building is required. A central space in this school building is the "home base". Students and staff of the same "home group" meet one another in the "living room" of the school every day. Ample room is available for (groups of) students to work on their projects. The school also contains a theatre, where projects can be presented, large groups can be taught together, and plays can be produced. It has a media and information space, a discovery room with a laboratory, a technical corner as well as an art corner. The building is designed for desk-independent computer usage.

## *Developing Slash/21*

Slash/21 was developed using futures thinking techniques of Business Process Redesign (BPR) from the world of business. It relied heavily on scenario-building, giving the process a strategic externally-focused orientation. The focus chosen was akin to the OECD scenario in which schools are seen as "Core Social Centres". However, while the OECD scenarios assume that change will happen as a consequence of tensions between societal demands and what schools are actually supplying, the designers of Slash/21 decided that they could intervene proactively. In this, they were like IBM when it decided it no longer worked in the business for office equipment but in the field of information processing, and introduced the personal computer. As one of the leading persons involved stated: "Society did not have to take over things: schools had to make a fundamental decision about the new business they were in."

"Business Process Redesign" is a technique where an organisation is designed as if it had to be built up for the first time. In comparing the existing organisation with the designed one, redundancy and illogical structures and processes can be traced which have grown into the organisation. Re-engineering an organisation starts from the most fundamental processes in the organisation: in schooling, this is learning. Taking the analogy with business one step further, the designers of Slash/21 were struck by the differences between the type of knowledge schools were offering and the types of knowledge the environment (*e.g.* employers) demands. Slash/21 was designed as a school where the focus was on tacit knowledge and knowledge structures rather than formal knowledge. The necessity of dealing with increasingly individualised children meant that the organisation was built up as a service organisation rather than a production organisation, with more flexibility and a greater sensitivity to demand.

Implementation of the concept was based on plans created by a business consultant, with intensive training of newly hired personnel and very intensive communication with parents and the local community.

## *Results*

Slash/21 was easily accepted by parents and the direct environment of the school. The message of the school was intensely communicated and understood by most parents. The school has been evaluated from the beginning by two universities in terms of reaching traditional cognitive objectives as well as the new objectives related to the Slash/21 concept. The Inspectorate has recently judged the school positively. The language curriculum – based on not more than one foreign language at one time, communicating for half the day in that language – has received a European Prize for curriculum innovation.

Innovations like Slash/21 are now replicated by around a dozen secondary schools in the Netherlands. They have had great influence on many more schools which were not totally redesigned but which introduced important elements of the original model – learning based on projects, not teacher-driven knowledge transfer; projects not based on subject-matter content; and schools with many non-teacher staff members working within the classroom.

In other sectors of education, there are comparable innovations to Slash/21, partly stimulated by its development. At the primary level, there is an increasing number of schools which organise learning processes fundamentally differently from the traditional system. There is a chain of schools with no formal curriculum, where pupil learning starts by their own motivation and energy. Many institutions of vocational education too are working on redesigning their education. Changes in the area of vocational education are characterised by the greater influence of local industries on the curriculum, competence as the basis for curriculum development, and more personalised learning inside and outside school. There are vocational institutions now with competence-based learning projects with almost no timetables and students working in learning communities, and without firm boundaries between secondary and tertiary (vocational) education for students with a weak theoretical orientation. These developments in turn may be expected in the long term to have an influence on secondary education.

While most schools in the Netherlands still operate more traditionally, re-designed schools are no longer perceived as strange phenomena but as realistic alternatives. On the other hand, there is a public debate on the effect of "new learning" on the cognitive skills of students. Primary education institutions which abolished the curriculum altogether tend to come in for particular criticism and the Dutch Inspectorate gave some of these school warnings for the lack of content in their (non-existent) curricula. Re-designing has sometimes become a goal in itself and thus no longer aimed at societal demands.

Scaling up the innovation is difficult because of a certain conservatism in society and because schools as professional organisations tend to resist change. In business chains, fundamental paradigm shifts are provoked by chain leaders, usually the elements of the business chain in direct contact with consumers. The school system has no "chain leader", especially in the Netherlands where the government has stopped playing this role.

## Conclusions

Considering the current governance philosophy and the reshuffling of responsibilities involved, the two initiatives described can be seen as valuable examples of the new steering paradigm in practice. Both innovation of the primary process of learning and teaching and developing school leadership are carried out by the professionals in the education field themselves instead of by the government. As a result, futures thinking is practised on the "shop floor" where it belongs. However, as this is still work in progress, there are important questions to be answered.

A first question is: how to encourage all schools to take greater pains over the development of the education they offer? While it may not be necessary for every school to complete a full makeover of themselves, all are obliged, with their main stakeholders, to establish a clear view on the future of their school and their contribution to the knowledge society. A second one is: how to enhance the effectiveness and efficiency of innovations? Do we want every school to re-invent the wheel for themselves? Or, is it possible to establish smart mechanisms through which schools can learn from each other? And how can we strengthen the relation between the education sciences and practitioners?

The theme for our continued participation in the OECD "Schooling for Tomorrow" project is "sharing knowledge for innovation", partly shaped by the experiences described above. Government still has the responsibility for the education system as a whole and the ways in which knowledge are produced, disseminated and applied in practice are crucial for the performance of the system. Therefore "sharing knowledge" will be the main issue for future Dutch work in this field in the coming years.

# Chapter 9
# New Zealand: the Secondary Futures project

*The New Zealand futures thinking initiative is working towards a vision for secondary education by: creating space to contemplate the future; providing tools to resource thinking about the future; sharing trends for the future direction of New Zealand society; sharing information about possibilities to make more students more successful; eliciting people's preferences in relation to the future of the New Zealand education system; supporting change by taking information out to others (all described in the chapter). This initiative has taken a unique approach to protecting the independence of the process by appointing four "guardians" with high profiles in the educational and non-educational fields.*

New Zealand has a national education system. In 2002, the Ministry of Education along with a newly elected government was interested in developing a broad-ranging discussion about what secondary schooling would be like in twenty years. Secondary Futures began after a strategy briefing by the Ministry of Education to the government highlighting the need to work with the schooling sector and the community to generate dialogue about the purpose and direction of secondary schooling. At the same time, there was a desire to focus the professional debate around the issues of quality teaching, student outcomes, and diversity issues. There was general consensus among education sector stakeholders that thinking about the future should be done in a structured approach and that this would be helped through participation in the OECD "Schooling for Tomorrow" project. The timescale for the New Zealand's Secondary Futures is for a period of up to twenty years ahead.

Secondary Futures helps New Zealanders create a vision for secondary education by:

- *Creating space* to contemplate the future.

- *Providing tools* to resource thinking about the future.
- *Sharing trends* for the future direction of New Zealand society.
- *Sharing information* about possibilities to make more students more successful.
- *Eliciting people's preferences* in relation to the future of the New Zealand education system.
- *Supporting change* by taking information out to others.

## Process design

The Secondary Futures Project was conceived by the New Zealand Ministry of Education and various sector stakeholders. New Zealand took a unique approach to group composition by appointing four *Guardians* with high profiles in the fields of tertiary and Mäori education, business innovation, education leadership, and sporting achievement. Their role was to protect the integrity and autonomy of the process. They were responsible for creating a space for dialogue by protecting the process from short-term policy and industry debates, a role foreseen to develop as the Guardians use their national profile to create networks and to install confidence in the project. They are aided by a small *secretariat team* autonomous from the Ministry of Education which provides the Guardians with access to research and information resources and to administrative support. There is also a *Touchstone Group* comprised mainly of NGOs which functions as a reference group and a conduit to key education sector organisations. Participation of culturally and professionally diverse groups has been encouraged and the debate on schooling widened to include new voices and participants. The major challenges include determining the best method of data collection for research and to use to effect change at local, national, and regional levels.

Like the original process which designed the OECD schooling scenarios, the Secondary Futures project has a critical desk-based aspect. The New Zealand government is interested in promoting futures projects in different sectors such as the labour market, immigration, sustainable business, biotechnology, and information and communications technology. The Secondary Futures project is working with these other projects on trends and values through which to analyse the context and opportunities for schooling in the future.

## Character narratives and the preference matrix

The focus of the Secondary Futures programme is on learners twenty years from now. The New Zealand project viewed the OECD scenarios as providing an opportunity to "leap into the future" and as a tool for group discussions. The scenarios were modified however, into frameworks that were accessible to New Zealand audiences (see box below). The new scenarios used less technical language while seeking to be faithful to the originals. Narratives of the various scenarios were developed that helped participants "walk in the shoes" of New Zealanders of the future.

## Step 1: interview with a citizen from 2025

Futures literacy is promoted through a simulated interview with a citizen from 2025. This activity introduces participants to futures language and approaches and allows them to brainstorm on what the future might look like.

## Step 2: original scenarios and role playing

The New Zealand research group felt that the "status quo" scenario was counter-productive to futures thinking by focusing people back to the present when the goal is to free them to imagine, having considered whether leaving this scenario out would distort or invalidate the responses to other scenarios. Similarly, the "meltdown" catastrophic scenario was not considered suitable. So, four of the OECD scenarios were adapted into frameworks that included concepts and key components that were interpreted in language that would be more accessible in a New Zealand setting. They were described as: *Social Centres*, *Focused Learning Centres, Networked Learning Society*, and *Individualised Choices* (see Box 9.1).

---

**Box 9.1. Secondary Futures Scenarios**

*Social Centres*. Many learning and personal development aims.

*Focused Learning Centres*. High value on information and knowledge.

*Networked Learning Society* where education is fully incorporated.

*Individual Choices*. A personalised model of learning in which individual choices shape what and how we learn.

---

A set of five roles or "personas", each of whom had a name, is developed – a learner, a learning facilitator/teacher, a parent, an employer, and a community leader/school administrator – and applied to each of the scenario frameworks. Narratives are then developed for each persona which allow participants to experience the future space, details of place, age, ethnicity, and family composition are included within each narrative.

*Step 3: a preference matrix*

Workshop participants then use a preference matrix in order to elicit prioritised preferences for each framework and determine a hierarchy of desirable features of schooling options.

*Step 4: dialogue*

The final step is an open dialogue about the future of education that draws on the experiential lessons from the previous stages.

## Further developments after the early design

*In the period since the Toronto Forum mid-2004, New Zealand's Secondary Futures project has made significant progress both with the development of resources for conducting a futures-focused conversation on possibilities for education, and with the organisation of information communicated as part of this conversation.*

### Participants

The Guardians and staff of the project have run workshops and addressed conferences all around New Zealand, predominantly in the education sector, and with youth audiences, as well as engaging with the business and community sector. A number of workshop formats have been devised, to accommodate different participants' needs. The optimum format takes place over a three-hour period, and gives participants sufficient time to start exploring preferences for the future of schooling. Secondary Futures has collected formal written feedback from, at the time of writing, over 900 participants in workshops, and engaged with hundreds more.

### Disengaging from the present

Secondary Futures considered feedback from the Toronto event around selecting only the re-schooling and de-schooling scenarios from the OECD

"Schooling for Tomorrow" project as the basis for discussion, and omitting the "status quo" scenarios. Pilot workshops held locally confirmed the earlier view that conditions in New Zealand were right for exploring alternatives to the bureaucratic school systems. The motivation behind the "status quo" scenarios, where "dissatisfaction does not reach the level where it precipitates real change" (Miller and Bentley, 2003, p. 29) was largely redundant for the New Zealand context.

A new activity, creating an "epitaph" for secondary education, has been introduced at the beginning of workshops. Participants are asked, "If secondary education died tomorrow, what would be its epitaph?" This provides a springboard for participants to disengage from today and acknowledge the desirability of exploring new possibilities. Overwhelmingly, epitaphs gathered from those working within the education sector, express negative perceptions of the current system. By reflecting on attitudes towards the current system and sharing these responses, participants are motivated to engage in a wide-ranging exploration of possibilities for the future.

## *Contemplating the future*

As part of the process of creating possibilities for education in the future, workshop participants requested help to first imagine a plausible future. While Secondary Futures is not in the business of predictions, the project has conducted extensive STEEP (social, technological, economic, environmental and political trends) analysis to ensure that all discussions regarding the future are grounded in plausible and credible trend information. From this scanning, a range of tools has been developed to stimulate thinking about what New Zealand might be like in twenty years.

A series of time-shift card has been created. These identify social, technological, economic, environmental and political snapshots twenty years ago and today – then prompt participants to think about how that trend might evolve in twenty years' time. These are predominantly a visual resource, servicing the project's mandate to bring a range of voices, including youth and a range of ethnic groups and people with low levels of literacy into the debate shaping education policy. Statistical trends, such as those around New Zealand's changing demographic profile, have been converted into a series of "possible" and "probable" trends cards. A series of "wildcards" have been created to suggest potential unforeseen jolts that might impact on the future of schooling. Having considered possibilities for the future of New Zealand society, participants are then invited to consider what a school leaver might need in order to be successful in this world.

## Deficiencies of the "frameworks"

Further trialling of the scenario frameworks suggested two fundamental flaws in the effectiveness of such detailed stories as a resource for futures thinking conversations:

- The first was that reading the framework was too time-consuming in workshops. There was also potential to exclude participants, on the basis of literacy, from the Secondary Futures conversation.

- The second was that the frameworks were too detailed too allow participants much scope for *imagining* the future; all imagining had been prescribed.

## Reworked scenarios

A series of "snapshot" scenarios, derived from the OECD's "Schools as Core Social Centres", "Schools as Focused Learning Organisations", "Learning Networks and the Network Society" and "Extending the Market Model", but summarised and adapted for New Zealand audiences, were produced. Known as the Blue, Red, Yellow and Green scenarios, these abbreviated scenarios allow participants sufficient information to imagine what each schooling experience might "look" like, and to take on the role of learners, teachers, parents, education and community leaders.

## Key questions

To create a vision for secondary education, broad questions need to be asked about the nature, purpose and form of secondary schooling and about the values and preferences New Zealanders have for the future. Independent research commissioned by Secondary Futures identified three key questions, posed in the context of twenty years hence:

- What is the purpose of secondary education?
- How can secondary education best enable young people for their futures?
- How could learning happen?

These questions provide an essential component of the research methodology for the evolving needs of the project.

## Building on the evidence of the Secondary Futures workshops

### *Key themes*

Having analysed hundreds of responses to the key questions, five clear "themes" have emerged that are fundamental to New Zealanders' vision for secondary education in the future.

### *a) "Students first"*

This theme explores student-centred learning, what it might look like, and what it would mean for organising and delivering secondary education in the future. Schooling moves away from a "one-size-fits-all" model, and places the goals, aspirations, and context of each student at the centre of delivery. In this vision, a student's dreams and talents are pivotal and defining: students articulate and lead their learning goals.

### *b) "Inspiring teachers"*

This theme investigates the re-definition of "teacher", moving away from the traditional role as leaders who transfer knowledge, to teachers as mentors, guides and facilitators working alongside learners. In this vision, more partnerships would occur and teachers would become more flexible, professional specialists.

### *c) "Social effects"*

This theme explores how future secondary education can enable students to achieve whatever outcomes are best suited to their context; who they are and where they come from. The outcomes of secondary education are multiple and layered. Success does not refer solely to academic outcomes. "Social" outcomes are at least as important. In this vision, secondary education enables young people to participate, to contribute, to succeed – as citizens, as part of the economy, as members of families, and part of communities.

### *d) "Community connectedness"*

This theme investigates preferences around how schooling and the community might connect in the future. Learning is more connected to the people and places outside the immediate school environment and harnesses all the resources of the community. In this vision, families, parents and industry and community leaders are all potential sources of knowledge, inspiration and role models who could enhance learning opportunities.

*e) "The place of technology"*

This theme examines preferences regarding the role of technology in future education. There is no doubt that technology will be influential in the organisation of schooling, though opinions about its impact range from optimism, to deep uncertainty and fear. Young people, for instance, worry that a technology-centred learning environment may come at the expense of social interaction.

## The matrix

The themes and key questions have been combined by Secondary Futures into a three-dimensional matrix.

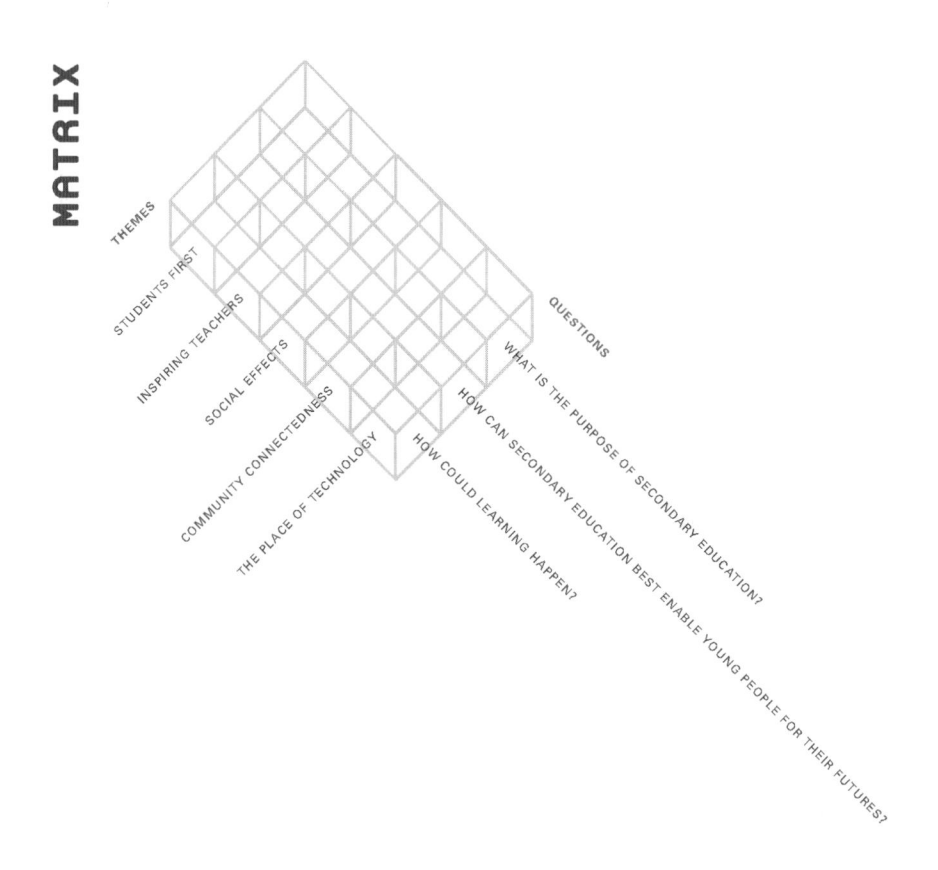

This matrix now provides the structure for ongoing conversations, investigations and analysis. It is intended that the matrix will provide a framework for organisation and analysis of the complex and multi-layered data which arises from our conversations. The matrix will also serve as a virtual filing cabinet – an online repository for information gathered during the course of the Secondary Futures conversation –, and as a reservoir of stimulus material to sustain and drive the conversation over the next two years.

## Related other projects

*"New schools" project:* Secondary Futures has initiated a project bringing the leaders of newly-formed schools together. Often, the freedom of a new site or new staff provides opportunities for these leaders to be innovative and work differently with learners. Yet a new site or staff is not necessary conditions for these changes. Secondary Futures is collecting stories from these schools and shares them with other schools, so they can consider how they might apply in their own communities. Barriers to change are identified, so that these might be addressed and avoided in the future. Secondary Futures then facilitates the exchange of this information with the state agencies that are in a position to dismantle these barriers.

*Supporting futures thinking capability:* Secondary Futures is also working with futures projects in the other public sectors to build futures thinking capability across a range of sectors.

# Feedback and reflection

As a result of extensive trialling and testing, Secondary Futures now has a toolbox of resources which can be used to systematically assist people to explore possible futures, the implications for education, and their preferences for schooling in the future. The process and tools are effective for developing capacity across a range of groups and sectors, including government, community and education, and building basic futures literacy. This capacity building has been widely acknowledged as both necessary and valuable in their current work.

Overwhelmingly, feedback from participants in workshops has endorsed the value of working with Secondary Futures to think about a distant future, the methodology, and the resources developed to stimulate rigorous imagining.

*"What have we learned?*

*We've learned that there's a lot of interest in our work.*

*That with help, people can think seriously about the future.*

*People we've worked with are starting to think outside the box they traditionally think in, extending their own networks, and working alongside others to think about how to get the best for students.*

*And some are starting to take an in-depth look at some future possibilities."*

(Mason Durie, Chair of the Secondary Futures Guardians, November 2004)

Secondary Futures has commissioned an external evaluation of the project's methodology and effectiveness to be conducted over the next three years. A report for stakeholders on how Secondary Futures has worked in 2004 is available on our website: *www.secondaryfutures.co.nz/pdfs/End_of_Year_Report.pdf*

# *Reference*

Miller, R. and T. Bentley (2003), "Unique Creation: Possible Futures; Four Scenarios for 21st Century Schooling", NCSL, Nottingham.

# Chapter 10
# Ontario (English-speaking system): the future of "Teaching as a Profession"

> *In the English-speaking school system in Ontario, the "Teaching as a Profession" initiative developed and adapted scenario tools for a series of workshops held with teachers, students, academics, principals, administrators, members of the private sector and civil servants. The new set of scenarios is: Redefining the Past, Breakdown, the Community-focused Model, Macro Models, and Breakthroughs in Complexity Science. The events promoted dialogue among the stakeholders after a tense period when dialogue and consensus had been difficult. The initiative showed the utility of futures scenarios in building policy capacity and in allowing for fruitful discussion on "teaching as a profession" among diverse groups of key individuals.*

## Introduction

This chapter begins with a brief description of the Ontario context, its educational system and the task at hand. It then analyses the Ontario research results distinguishing goals, process design, and scenario content. It draws some initial conclusions on outcomes and benefits of futures thinking, and describes the beginnings of the next phase of the English language Ontario project.

In Ontario the first two phases of the "Teaching as a Profession" work concentrated on examining the utility of futures scenarios in building policy capacity and in allowing for fruitful and open discussion on the topic of "Teaching as a Profession" among diverse groups of individuals. Workshops were held with teachers, students, academics, principals, administrators, members of the private sector and civil servants. They illustrated that scenarios are useful in enabling discussion, allowing individuals to think about the future in a different light and in opening people's minds to be receptive of new perspectives.

The next phase of the project will seek to apply the scenarios to Canadian policy issues by using mature case studies and futures scenarios together. The hope is that by jointly connecting actual historic case studies from other jurisdictions with futures thinking and then applying the discussion to current Ontario policy issues, the quality of Ontario's policy development related to similar issues will be enhanced.

## The reform context

The changing role of schools and schooling is a major concern to most OECD jurisdictions, including Ontario. There are many perspectives on the purpose of education, each of which prescribes differing roles and status for teaching and schools. Diverse visions of what education is supposed to accomplish include: preparation for work, personal development, transmission of a cultural heritage and other values. Similarly, teachers are also characterised in a variety of ways: from unionised workers to highly specialised professionals. The combination of these different factors results in a complex environment in which it is often difficult to achieve meaningful dialogue, let alone consensus. In recent decades, citizens in most jurisdictions have sought greater assurance that their schools are graduating properly-educated young people. As a result, intense efforts at education reform have taken place worldwide over the last 20 years or so.

Many of the reform attempts have been directed toward such areas as curriculum, early childhood education, assessment, accountability, and graduation requirements. Particularly over the past decade, education reforms have been largely standards- and results-based, with an emphasis on accountability. In Ontario, these reforms included a new curriculum for kindergarten to grade 12, a new emphasis on literacy and numeracy, standardised testing of students in Math and English, a mandatory "learning to age 18" strategy, a funding mechanism for school boards that provides a similar level of per pupil funding regardless of local tax base, standardised report cards, and greater and more meaningful parental involvement. The Ontario College of Teachers, a self-regulating professional body for Ontario's teachers, was also created in 1996.

Given the vital role teachers play in enhancing student outcomes, teaching and teacher education is an integral part of recent education reform efforts. Ontario's contribution to teaching reform has resulted in a set of initiatives aimed at supporting teachers and quality teaching. These initiatives include a teacher induction programme, enhanced supports for teacher professional development, an entry to the teaching profession assessment for new teachers, a provincial teacher performance appraisal system (for evaluating teachers), and teaching excellence awards. (An additional reform brought in by a previous Ontario government that mandated professional development requirements for teachers was the subject of intense debate and controversy and has recently been revoked.)

## The task

Governments and educational sector stakeholders invest valuable time, effort, and resources in their efforts to effect change and improve the education system. How can educational sector managers and stakeholders be convinced that the efforts that are being made today will meet the needs of tomorrow? This question resonates even more so when one takes into consideration that educational systems were developed to meet the needs of an industrial society. Today, as OECD countries move rapidly towards a knowledge society with its demands for a new model of the educated citizen, decision makers must make strategic choices to reform the educational system so that the youth of today can meet the challenges of tomorrow. Thus, it is useful to determine whether or not futures thinking adds to the policy choices and decisions faced by educational systems in anticipating the future education needs of an evolving, ever-changing society.

In Ontario, the initial task became to stimulate dialogue on the issue of teachers and the teaching profession and to build policy capacity. Ontario developed and utilised modified OECD scenarios to begin to address several issues, including:

- How does the issue of teachers as professionals relate to the quality of teaching?
- In order to maximise student learning and achievement, what would the status of the teaching profession be under the various scenarios?
- Should teachers be treated the same as other professionals?

The Ontario project uses "alternative futures" as an integral contribution to discussion. The methodology is based on a multiple-scenarios strategic planning framework that identifies desirable futures and the strategies for achieving them. The starting point for dialogue was the series of futures developed by the OECD.

Over the course of the project, Ontario has engaged an increasingly wide variety of experts, teachers and others with an interest in education in order to clarify how various alternative ideas about schools and schooling will have consequences relating to teaching as a profession. It is anticipated that this process will allow a series of preferred scenarios to emerge, will enable the development of robust strategies to further policy discussion and decision-making, and build greater understanding.

The Ontario project is currently entering its third phase, which will continue to explore the issue of teaching as a profession and to identify and clarify how scenarios can act as a new methodology to support discussion and policy decision-making. This new phase also focuses on whether examining historic case studies of real policy issues, in tandem with examining the same issue using futures scenarios, can further enhance policy-making and allow for greater understanding of the contextual issues that can come into play in policy analysis, development and implementation.

## The Ontario system

With a population of more than 12 million, Ontario is home to about 39% of the country's population, roughly one in three Canadians. Eighty per cent of the province's population live in urban centres, largely in cities on the shores of the Great Lakes. The economy of northern Ontario is highly dependent on natural resources, while southern Ontario is heavily industrialized, largely because of its proximity to the U.S. market. Contributing about 40% of Canada's total employment, employment in Ontario has shifted largely to the service industries, namely business services, finance, tourism and culture in recent years rather than on assembly lines.

Ontario's population growth has always been largely dependent on immigration. Today, Ontario is one of the most ethnically diverse jurisdictions in the world. Almost half of the approximately 250 000 people who immigrate to Canada each year choose to settle in Ontario. Toronto, the largest city in Canada, has been called the most multicultural city in the world, where more than 70 languages are spoken.

In Ontario, all permanent residents between the ages of 6 and 16 must attend school. The Ontario Ministry of Education is responsible for education from kindergarten through Grade 12. It develops curriculum policy, sets provincial standards for student performance, evaluates and approves learning materials for use in schools, allocates funds for the system, reports results to the public, and oversees the system's governance.

Ontario has a dual-system of publicly funded education, distinguished by language (English, French) and religion (non-denominational, Catholic). While English is Ontario's official language, French language rights have been extended to the legal and educational systems. Most of Ontario's two million elementary and secondary school students study in English, however approximately 100 000 of these students have French as a first language and study in the French system. There are approximately 120 000 certified teachers, of which 105 000 teach in a classroom setting and the remaining hold various administrative positions.

A publicly-funded education system, Ontario's school boards operate and administer their schools using funding received from the province. Ontario's 72 District School Boards are made up of 31 English-language public boards, 29 English-language Catholic boards, 4 French-language public boards, and 8 French-language Catholic boards. As well, a small number of Ontario schools are operated by School Authorities which manage special types of schools, such as schools in hospitals and treatment facilities, and schools in remote and sparsely populated regions.

At the time of the engagement with the OECD "Schooling for Tomorrow" project, Ontario's education system was in the midst of heightened levels of tension. The government then in power was trying to deliver on an education agenda of which the content and manner of implementation were unpopular with most education stakeholders, especially teachers. The positions of various education stakeholders had become polarised and entrenched, with great suspicion of government motives and initiatives. The OECD "Schooling for Tomorrow" project was viewed by the Ministry as an opportunity to promote "safe" discussion and expand thinking about the topic of "Teaching as a Profession" with a diverse group of education stakeholders and other interested individuals.

In the fall 2004, a new Ontario government was elected. Since then many changes have occurred and significant steps have been taken which have improved government relations with teachers, school boards and other education stakeholders. The issue of "Teaching as a Profession" remains relevant. The current government specifically campaigned on a platform of enhanced respect for teachers. The government is also currently in the process of revitalising the Ontario College of Teachers, the self-governing entity for teachers.

## The goals of the initiatives

The OECD project provides an opportunity to foster discussion about teachers and education amongst individuals within the education sector and beyond. In addition to exploring the value of scenarios to policy development, the aim has been to use the futures scenarios provided by the OECD to help individuals expand their thinking, and expand the thinking, values and beliefs of their organisations and sectors; as well as to reflect on the future of teachers and teaching in Ontario. To this end, the project's initial goals focused on capacity building and the promotion of multiple perspectives, rather than necessarily solutions to policy issues. As the project has evolved, Ontario has become more focused on enhancing the quality of policy development and capacity by exploring new methodology through the use of futures scenarios in conjunction with other mechanisms (*e.g.* case studies).

## Process design

### *Phases 1 and 2*

One of the first steps taken by the Ontario Ministry of Education was to hire researchers to conduct a literature review on the topic "Teaching as a Profession". Next, a core study group was created to act as a project advisory panel. Twelve diverse external and internal education experts of varying backgrounds – including educators, bureaucrats, administrators, academics, lawyers, political advisors and union leaders – were invited to form the study team for the project. This group tested out the scenarios and the workshop plans. A research team, with experience in futures scenario planning, was also hired at the end of 2002.

At the first study group meeting, the study team worked with the OECD's six scenarios. We found that the specificity with respect to the role of teachers in each of the OECD's scenarios impeded the scope of the conversation and dialogue, so the research team modified the scenarios to fit the purposes of the Ontario project and to meet the needs of the study group. The revised scenarios were written to be as broad as possible and to provide a set of social, political and economic environments within which to discuss the role of teachers. Background charts were created in order to build the necessary context. The charts examined the effects of multiple variables across each scenario, describing, for example, the focus of governing power (as one variable) in each scenario. Once the charts had been completed, the differences between the scenarios were exaggerated to create five highly differentiated futures. The new scenarios made little or no mention of education, as the intention was to provide a general framework within which to discuss the future of teaching and teaching as a profession. Once the study group had worked with five modified scenarios, and became comfortable with them, the process of organising larger workshops began.

Of the workshops, some were made up primarily of individuals from various organisations and sectors and some were made up of groups representing similar organisations/interests (*i.e.*, teaching regulators, Ministry of Education employees). Approximately 150 people, from across the education and other sectors, have taken part in the project up to 2005.

The original workshop programme was based on a seven-hour time frame. In the morning, participants were divided into groups of five or six and each group was assigned one of the scenarios to discuss and asked to focus on the question: "What would teachers and teaching look like in this future?" In the afternoon, the participants moved on to a second scenario and endeavoured to isolate some actions that would maximise the positive aspects and minimise the negative aspects of the scenario. The selection of participants for the workshops was largely based upon recommendations of the study team and previous workshop participants. Three of the workshops were purposely composed of individuals of varying interests and backgrounds. These groups were geographically and sectorally diverse, with individuals from various constituencies and positions within sectors such as education, labour, health and communications attending from across Canada, as well as from the United States.

In response to feedback from the early workshops, the workshop structure of the "Teaching as a Profession" discussion was changed. After March 2003, participants commented that they would like an opportunity to work with all five scenarios instead of just two. At the next workshop, the afternoon was modified to allow everyone to deal with all the scenarios. The scenarios were further modified as the project progressed. To focus the conversations on teaching, texts were added to the scenarios to describe the educational environment. A list of targeted questions was provided to each group in order to better focus the discussion on the specific education issues Ontario wished to explore. The charts on which the scenarios had been based were distributed to participants along with the scenarios. This appeared to increase people's confidence in the scenarios.

One of the distinctive aspects of the "Teaching as a Profession" model was the use of voting. At the beginning of each workshop, participants were asked to vote on the scenario that they believed to be most likely as well as on the scenario that they preferred, with the idea of determining: i) whether votes were distributed evenly among the groups; and ii) to introduce the difference between preference and likelihood. At the end of the day, a second vote was taken to determine if people's opinions had shifted (see Table 10.1 below). Although the results demonstrate that this occurred only to some degree, at individual meetings, there were often marked shifts between the first and second rounds of voting. Even though it did not occur at all the meetings, a shift was regarded as a positive sign in showing how the use of scenarios could open up people's thinking. Voting therefore served as a tool to facilitate discussion and to challenge previously-entrenched ideas and it helped to provide evidence that *the use of scenarios can successfully open up or expand people's thinking.*

The questionnaire results from the Phase 1 and 2 workshops produced the following outcomes:

**Table 10.1. Workshop responses to the scenarios**

|  | Preferred (round one) | Preferred (round two) | Most likely (round one) | Most likely (round two) |
|---|---|---|---|---|
| 1 – Refining the past | 31 | 33 | 50 | 51 |
| 2 – Breakdown | 0 | 2 | 7 | 4 |
| 3 – Community focused model | 35 | 23 | 6 | 13 |
| 4 – Macro-markets | 12 | 11 | 45 | 23 |
| 5 – Complexity | 47 | 36 | 17 | 14 |

## *Phase 3*

A third phase has recently been initiated. It is intended to further evolve the range of futures methods and pursue discussions to directly address policy questions related to teaching as a profession, by considering case studies from the past, scenarios for the future, and applying them to policy development in the present. Three case studies were commissioned to examine the social, economic and political circumstances of three school-related policies that had been implemented in other provinces in Canada. By using these case studies, we are better able to understand the context within which policy decisions are made. The topics of the case studies are:

- Mandatory School Attendance (New Brunswick)
- Provincial Student Assessment (British Columbia)
- Open School Catchment Boundaries (British Columbia)

A workshop was designed to submit the case studies to discussion using futures scenarios as a vehicle and a pilot workshop used Study Group members as participants. It considered the New Brunswick Mandatory School Attendance policy which raised the school leaving age from 16 to 18. In the morning, participants were asked to examine this policy in the context of each of the five scenarios using the following questions: "Would this policy make sense in this scenario?" "How would you change it?" "How would the policy affect teachers and teaching in this scenario?" and "What other policies would you consider or introduce in this scenario?" The discussion led to unexpected insights into the nature of the policy and some of its consequences. For example, in some scenarios, there was no adolescent age at which school leaving could be set because of requirements for lifelong learning. In others, the formal school leaving age might have to be lowered to allow students more opportunity to work in conjunction with their education.

In the afternoon there was a detailed and lively elaboration of the case study, which explored its place in the social, economic and political context of New Brunswick at the time. The participants were then asked to adopt a role (not their own) while they discussed the two following questions:

- Assume you belong to a particular interest group (*e.g.* teachers) and that you live in New Brunswick in the future (*e.g.* Scenario 1). Looking back to the 1990s when the Mandatory School Attendance policy was being developed, and given what you know about the future, how would you have changed the position you took on this policy in the 1990s?

- Assume you belong to a particular interest group (*e.g.* teachers) and that you live in New Brunswick in the 1990s. You have knowledge on what the future is going to look like (*e.g.* Scenario 1). Given your knowledge of what the future is like, how would it influence your position on a Mandatory School Attendance policy that is currently being developed (*i.e.* in the 1990s)?

Feedback from the pilot workshop indicated that utilising case studies, as well as futures scenarios, was extremely useful and stimulating in terms of generating discussion. As a result of lessons learned from the pilot workshop, a new workshop has been devised which begins with a discussion of a case study, and then asks the questions used in the morning of Workshop 1 and ends with lessons for current policy discussions. This workshop will be the first of a series to connect historical case studies (past) to scenarios (futures) in policy discussions (present).

## Scenario content

Ontario's "Teaching as a Profession" used modified scenarios (see Box 10.1) as a basis for discussion. The five alternative scenarios illustrate differing impacts on teachers' roles in Ontario thirty years into the future. They have been constructed to differentiate possible roles for teachers and perspectives on teaching in the long term. The schooling alternatives were developed by a group of researchers in Ontario in order to provide a basis for exploring possible ways of teaching in the future.

The scenarios are differentiated using a number of parameters. For example, the macro-market future does not depend on continuing political rule by international market advocates. Instead it considers that these attitudes will predominate everywhere so that all political parties will assume policies in the direction of those indicated. Some factors are projected in all five futures but there may still be variations of emphasis. In all scenarios, there are important advances in the understanding of education: a more fundamental knowledge about many developmental processes and influences on learning and capacity. But these occur at differing times and with differing impacts in the different scenarios.

---

**Box 10.1. The Ontario "Teaching as a Profession" scenarios in brief**

*Refining the past.* This future brings new evidence and experience to the structures and processes of the early 21$^{st}$ century. Canadian civil federalism becomes a preferred world model. Governing systems become far more efficient and accountable and the mixed public/private economy is regulated to produce slow and steady growth. The educational system is highly regulated in terms of curriculum, credentials, and accountability for results.

*Breakdown.* This is a depressed and unstable future with a very high level of unemployment and underemployment. Warfare and terrorism increase the number of refugees, and international trade becomes difficult. Technological innovation supports effective, low-cost ways of delivering no-frills service. Public education systems break down, become smaller, are chronically under-funded and less comprehensive. Alternative forms of schooling increase.

*Community focused model.* This future emphasises the impact of changes in the nature of community life. Community life changes dramatically with an increase in the concern for the environment. Large numbers of self-sustaining communities develop strong local cultures and are responsible for educating their own members.

*Macro models.* This future maximises the long-term impacts of global trade. Major global businesses increase dramatically in number and scale and the boundaries between corporate and national interests become blurred. The importance of knowledge management is recognised in both the public and private sector as essential to development. Lifelong learning becomes common for everyone.

*Major breakthroughs in complexity science.* Complex systems develop with linked social, economic, and political growth tied to access to "learning by doing". Multi-faceted learning networks are possible due to communication and transportation capacity provided by technology. Lifelong learning is encouraged.

# Outcomes and benefits

## *Benefits of futures thinking*

A number of important lessons have emerged from experiences. The scenarios proved to be an effective way of opening up people's thinking and moving them away from entrenched biases and viewpoints. Using the scenarios also gave participants the opportunity to discuss certain issues in education in an open environment. People felt that they were able to talk about education with individuals in a setting and manner in which they would never normally have the opportunity. One participant said, "I find the scenarios have helped me broaden my thinking. I find myself slipping back at times but at least now I can identify when I'm being narrow-minded. I find it interesting and informative to be able to hear other people's points of view and to have the experience to work with a group of such a wide variety of backgrounds is very enriching". Another participant found that "when you speculate, you generate options to create". There was great enthusiasm about the project for those reasons.

## *Limitations of futures thinking*

Many participants felt that there are limitations to the use of futures scenarios generally and the use of particular futures scenarios in policy development. One such person wrote, "Policies reflect the contexts in which they arise, including the traditions, values, institutions, resources, etc., that characterise those contexts… The scenarios … are insufficiently sensitive to context for the purpose of policy development". Overall the project, up until this point, has shown that scenarios are useful for promoting discussions, but there may be limits to their usefulness in policy development, particularly because they can never fully capture the contextual and situational importance in which policy is designed, decided upon and delivered. Through the introduction of a case study approach, the current phase of the project is intended to bring the scenarios closer to current policy issues that face schools in Ontario.

## *Lessons learnt for policy development*

The Ontario project has been a success and shown quite clearly that futures scenarios can be effective in opening up discussion among competing groups on a contentious issue such as the future of teaching as a profession. The use of future scenarios allowed such disparate participants as union leaders, parents, school administrators, teachers, and civil servants to engage in discussion without falling into traditional postures. Almost all showed a capacity to explore the issues in depth considering a range of future possibilities, most changed their minds about the future they preferred and some changed their minds about which was most likely. This was demonstrated by the very positive feedback received from the post-workshop discussions (see Table 10.2 below).

**Table 10.2. Evaluation of the process by workshop participants**

|  | 1(worst) | 2 | 3 | 4 | 5 (best) |
|---|---|---|---|---|---|
| What was your overall impression of the workshop? | 0 | 0 | 5 | 35 | 50 |
| Please rate how useful you found the scenarios in expanding your thinking. | 0 | 0 | 11 | 41 | 38 |
| Please rate the potential utility of the scenarios in policy development. | 0 | 3 | 14 | 33 | 38 |
| How did you feel about the length of the workshop? | Too long 5 | X | Just right 66 | X | Too short 19 |

Results from these workshops have led us to conclude that futures scenarios can be useful in opening up policy discussion among diverse groups on difficult topics.

In the new phase we are attempting to consider the connections between future, past and present policy concerns. We have commissioned three case studies of past policy initiatives. We are designing workshops that relate these to future scenarios with a view to their application to current policy issues. We have so far drawn no conclusions, but look forward to the development of a product that can help participants understand more about the process of policy development and improve participation in actual policy debate.

# Chapter 11
# Ontario (French-speaking system): the *Vision 2020* initiative[1]

> *The* Vision 2020 *initiative has proved to be timely given that Ontario's francophones had gained access to school governance at the end of the 1990s yet amidst concern about assimilation and the erosion of their unique culture. The Ministry, French-language educational institutions, and the various partners in education, felt the need to assess their progress, define the challenges they face in delivering quality French-language education, and reflect on the future of French-language education in Ontario – all of which the* Vision 2020 *initiative has achieved. From a starting point of the OECD six schooling scenarios, this initiative has worked towards its own seventh vision and scenario of the future of French-language schooling. Young people have provided a particular feature of the stakeholder involvement.*

## Introduction and background

This chapter provides an overview of the *Vision 2020* initiative, developed by the Ontario Ministry of Education in the fall of 2002 under the auspices of OECD. The ministry decided to run two parallel "Schooling for Tomorrow" initiatives, one in English (see Chapter 10) and this one in French, named *Vision 2020*.

Developed and implemented by the Ministry's French-Language Education Policy and Programs Branch, *Vision 2020* was both timely and appropriate to the needs of the province, six years after Ontario's francophones had gained access to school governance. At this time, the Ministry, French-language educational institutions, and the various partners

---

[1] Prepared by Monique Gauvin, Consulting Sociologist for the Ministry of Education, Ontario, Canada French-Language Education Policy and ProgRams Branch.

in education, felt the need to assess their progress, define the challenges they face in delivering quality French-language education, and reflect on the future of French-language education in Ontario. The *Vision 2020* initiative provided an ideal platform for this reflection

## The provincial context

Ontario's education system is sub-divided into four school systems: English-language public, English-language Catholic, French-language public and French-language Catholic. In 1998, distinct (Catholic and public) school systems were established for Ontario's francophone community. School governance has made it possible for francophone parents to gain more control over their schools through French-language school boards, and many new schools have been opened.

The francophone minority is nevertheless concerned about assimilation and the erosion of its unique culture. The threat of assimilation is the principal challenge facing the half-million Franco-Ontarian community and living in a minority environment is similar to the situation faced globally by minority communities:

- Marginalisation and erosion of their linguistic and cultural space.
- Low francophone birth rates.
- The arrival of immigrants, a great majority of whom adopt English on their arrival in Canada (nine out of 10 immigrants adopt English).
- Rising rates of exogamous marriage.
- A small francophone population representing about 4.5% of the total population.
- Distribution of the francophone community across a geographically large and predominantly Anglophone population.
- Saturation by English-language media.

These factors contribute to the uncertainty surrounding the long-term continuity of Ontario's French-language community. In this context, schools must respond to formidable challenges with respect to transmission of the language, building of a francophone identity, appropriation of the culture, fostering academic performance and success in a minority environment, and recruitment and retention of those students who have the right to receive instruction in the minority language.

Given this context and these challenges, *Vision 2020* participants have been especially sensitive to the issues implicit in the OECD scenarios with respect to the very future of schooling in the larger context of changes that are occurring internationally. The OECD "Schooling for Tomorrow" project and its scenarios have provided an ideal opportunity to undertake reflection on the future of French-language education in Ontario.

## Goals of the initiative

The key objective of *Vision 2020* is to establish a dialogue involving the Ministry of Education, education partners, and representatives of the "new generation", aimed at the development of a shared vision of French-language education in Ontario, and joint strategies for achieving it.

Francophone school governance was established as a result of claims from the French-language community that were ultimately successful. The challenge now is to enable the various education partners to move beyond this stage, and shift their focus toward developing this system's capacity to reflect on its long-term development, and engage in open discussion on a matter of public policy with respect to its own vitality and survival. It must ask itself the question: what kind of French-language school do we want in the future? Such a question also calls for an assessment of the methods to be used to define the parameters of the French-language school of tomorrow.

The scenario-based approach to visualising the parameters of the school of the future has proved valuable as a means to develop the capacity to think about the future, in part because it challenges our tendency to perceive the majority model as the ideal model both in the present and for the future. The approach provides an opportunity to consider other options for the school of tomorrow. In addition, forward-thinking challenges the concepts and expectations that limit our ability to act in the present.

## Process and implementation

### *Process development*

The current *Vision 2020* scenario-based approach was developed through three phases. Throughout the process, scenarios have been used to open discussion and free participants from everyday concerns that might prevent them from seeing desirable futures.

In the first phase of *Vision 2020* an Expert Panel was formed. During this phase, participants familiarised themselves with the forward-thinking approach by considering the question, "If any of the six OECD scenarios prevailed, what impact would each scenario have on francophone school governance and, specifically, on the French-language school?" Discussions considered topics such as the governance of French-language schools, cooperative structures for the public and Catholic components of the system, administrative models for the recruitment of educators and the nature of parent and community participation. In the second phase, through most of 2003, scenarios implicit in the Ministry's *Aménagement linguistique* (language planning) policy were compared with the OECD scenarios. In the third phase of the project since then, the OECD scenarios were explored with groups representing the "new generation" of students, young parents and teachers, through a filter of individual and shared values in order to develop a seventh scenario for the French-language School of the Future.

## *Scenario content*

The design process for *Vision 2020* was slow and deliberate, in order to build capacity and encourage dialogue. Responses to initial discussions by Ministry representatives and members of the Expert Panel led to significant changes to the project. Firstly, Panel members wanted more time to examine the OECD scenarios, so summaries and an analytical framework were developed to help them do this, with a focus on governance in the future.

Secondly, the members of the Expert Panel and a group of francophones from various Ontario government ministries began exploring the links between the scenario-based approach and the process used to develop public policy, in this case the Government of Ontario's *Aménagement linguistique* (language planning) policy, which was being developed at the time.

In doing so, participants noted the scenario-based approach's limitations in taking context into account, especially challenges faced by minority communities, and linguistic and cultural issues. Phase III of *Vision 2020* has been developed in order to give this context greater consideration.

## *Workshop development in the third phase*

The *Fédération de la jeunesse franco-ontarienne* (FESFO), which has considerable expertise in youth facilitation, was key to the design of this third phase. An agreement was reached between the Ministry of Education and the FESFO concerning the approach, facilitation formula and logistics of organising a workshop for young Franco-Ontarians. The approach used in that workshop has been used and continuously improved in subsequent ones during 2004 and 2005 with groups of the "new generation" and education partners and is described below.

In the *Vision 2020* workshops, activities are focused on the "Schooling for Tomorrow" scenarios published by the OECD in 2001. The participants take ownership of the scenarios through a series of facilitated discussions or steps which last 12-15 hours over two or three days:

- *Step 1: Identification of values:* Participants use the facilitation tool developed by FESFO to identify their own values and the values shared by the group for the French-language School of the Future.

- *Step 2: Scenario work:* Using a facilitation framework developed by FESFO and the Ministry, the participants are divided into six groups. Each group is asked to carry out an in-depth analysis of one of the six OECD scenarios and to become expert in this scenario. The participants are asked to identify the advantages and challenges of such a scenario, the winners and losers, and the values inherent in the scenario under discussion, and to evaluate the impact of such a scenario on the French-language school. The members of each group are then asked to develop their own stories based on the scenario they have explored, and to present the scenario to all of the other participants, in the plenary session, in the form of a sketch or some other kind of presentation.

- *Step 3: The seventh scenario:* Lastly, the participants are divided into sub-groups and asked to develop a seventh scenario that describes the parameters of the French-language School of the Future based on their essential values. Each sub-group then presents or describes its seventh scenario to the other participants during a final plenary session. The desired outcome of this step, and ultimately of the project, is the development of a shared vision of the desirable future for French-language education in Ontario.

## Outcomes and analysis

The overall outcomes of the *Vision 2020* project cannot be evaluated until a comparative and cumulative analysis of the content of all of the consultations has been carried out at the end of the process, which is expected to conclude by the end of 2006. Consequently, the observations reflected here are preliminary.

We believe the *Vision 2020* project is leading toward the development of a vision for French-language schooling in 2020, in part through the workshop approach developed during the project. This approach, which is based on shared values, enables us not only to further explore the OECD scenarios but to develop a seventh scenario for the French-language School of the Future, based on values that are considered essential and desirable by the participants.

After initial testing of the approach with a groups of approximately 25 each of young people, parents, and teachers throughout 2004, we updated the facilitation formula for use with groups (again of approximately 25 each) of French-language school principals and directors of education and school board trustees in the first half of 2005. During the process, we compared the "visions" that emerged from each group to verify the extent of their complementarity. In subsequent work, we would like to test the approach with heterogeneous regional groups to obtain the perspective of the broader francophone community concerning the desirable school of the future.

## The learning process

Among the observable outcomes of Phase III of *Vision 2020* is the fact that the project is becoming a significant consultation initiative, both because of the number of consultations that will have taken place by late 2006 and because of the number of people consulted. In addition, consultation-planning tools and research tools for analysing the content of these consultations, and changes to the facilitation process, began to be developed at the end of 2004. We are also beginning work on a *Vision 2020* Facilitation and Consultation Kit to help education partners and community agencies take ownership of the consultation process, and we hope to have the kit available towards the end of 2006.

## Learning through an inclusive and experimental approach

The challenge of the consultation and facilitation approach adopted in the *Vision 2020* project was to encourage the participants to take ownership of the process, which consists of creating a seventh scenario for the French-language School of the Future that takes the shared values into consideration. We believe we have now assembled the successful conditions for such ownership.

## The appropriateness and benefits of an inclusive approach

The adoption of an inclusive approach – from the grassroots to the decision makers and encompassing those who study, teach, administer and manage within the French-language education system – is based on the premise that change in the French-language education system cannot be conceived of solely as a movement that trickles down from the top of the hierarchy to the bottom. The adoption by *Vision 2020* of an inclusive approach that begins with those at the base of the hierarchy has so far been very favourably received by the participants. For example, some adults said they appreciated the fact that young people were consulted first, and some young people felt valued because their point of view was considered. Asking partner organisations to help with the recruitment of participants gave these organisations an opportunity not only to see members of their "new generation" in action, but also to assess the appropriateness of the consultation and facilitation process on site and take part in its ongoing evaluation.

The approach which has been adopted is also supported by the idea that no education system in a minority environment can be developed, and no reflection on its future can be conceived of, without the perspective and contribution of the community it is meant to serve. This approach reflects the spirit of the *Aménagement linguistique* policy[2] which has been implemented by the Ontario Ministry of Education. In this respect, *Vision 2020* is contributing, as far as possible, to all stakeholders' involvement in reflection on the future of French-language education in Ontario.

### *The partnership between the Ministry and the* Fédération de la jeunesse franco-ontarienne *(FESFO)*

One aspect of the latter phase of *Vision 2020* was the creation of a partnership between the Ministry of Education and the *Fédération de la jeunesse franco-ontarienne* (FESFO) to establish a model for the forthcoming consultations and organise these consultations. The partnership between the Ministry Working Group (which coordinates logistics and research) and the FESFO (which takes part in recruitment and is responsible for facilitation) has proved to be highly productive. Having a third party assuming responsibility for facilitation frees the Ministry to listen to and analyse the consultation sessions, and enables the young people and adults who are being consulted to experience a facilitation and consultation process that has been developed primarily by FESFO.

---

[2] The Ontario Ministry of Education's *Politique d'aménagement linguistique de l'Ontario pour l'éducation en langue française* (*Aménagement linguistique – A Policy for Ontario's French-Language Schools and Francophone Community*) was officially released in October 2004.

## *The limitations of the scenario-based approach*

We have found that the OECD scenarios do have certain limitations in their capacity to encourage forward-thinking, limitations that were in fact noted by several of the jurisdictions that took part in the OECD "Schooling for Tomorrow" project. With respect to *Vision 2020*, we have seen that the participants in the *Vision 2020* forums perceived several of the scenarios to be more relevant to the present than to the future. And, in fact, the forward-thinking indicators in the *Vision 2020* project look ahead 20 years or less, to the relatively near future.

In view of such considerations, the facilitators have made a special effort to encourage workshop participants to look beyond their present-day concerns and do their utmost to see themselves in 2020. To better prepare the participants, a visualisation exercise has been introduced at the start of the consultation, during an icebreaker session. The participants are encouraged to introduce themselves, to tell the others where they were 15 years ago, to assess the most important change that has occurred since then and to evaluate what, in their opinion, has been the most important change in the past 15 years.

## *Evaluation of the consultation and facilitation approach*

During the third phase of *Vision 2020*, we were able to confirm whether or not we were on the right track by means of ongoing evaluation of the facilitation process used by FESFO through the inclusion of evaluation questions in the participants' guide and the facilitators' guide, and an evaluation session for the main organisers at the end of every consultation. *Vision 2020* has embarked on a process of continuous improvement from one consultation to the next, drawing on aspects considered positive as well as criticisms made by participants and organisers after each consultation concerning aspects such as the method used to analyse and explore the scenario content, the facilitation approach and quality, and the choice of facilitators for each consultation. At the same time certain basic elements used to compare the results of the various *Vision 2020* forums have been retained.

## *Learning through participant ownership of the process*

The challenge of the facilitation approach was to enable the participants to take ownership of the process of analysing and further exploring the OECD scenarios and creating a seventh scenario for the French-language School of the Future. Within the framework of the process that was used, the participants were able to:

- Identify both their individual values and the values that they as a group consider to be those of the French-language schools.

- Analyse and further explore the OECD scenarios, reflect on the values inherent in the scenarios, the advantages and disadvantages or challenges posed by the scenarios, identify the winners and losers in each scenario, thereby recognising the realities of others in the scenario, whether they be students, teachers, parents, administrators, etc.

- Imagine themselves as a group in a given scenario because the participants were encouraged to ask themselves questions about the scenario's impact on the francophone and, specifically, French-language schools and the French-language education.

- Identify those values they consider essential and desirable and develop a seventh scenario for the French-language School of the Future by mapping the desired scenario with reference also to people who have parental responsibilities, who are studying, teaching or acting as administrators, to design a structure for a French-language education system in the desired scenario, the distribution of power in such a scenario, and so on.

In general, the participants tend to appreciate the weekend they have spent reflecting on the French-language School of the Future. Based on the consultations that began early in 2004 and have been analysed thus far, and on the evaluations submitted by participants in the consultations that have already been carried out, the participants:

- Feel they have experienced an authentic consultation process in which they feel respected.

- Generally say that they appreciated the Ministry's attentiveness and felt their opinion counted.

- Say they appreciated the facilitation skills and professionalism of the *Fédération de la jeunesse franco-ontarienne* (FESFO).

- Appreciate the opportunity to explore their personal values (a time for reflection that they do not often have at school) and to identify the values they share with others by identifying as a group the French-language School of the Future; in their evaluations many of them stated that they appreciated the opportunity to realise they were not the only ones who felt like they do.

- Are aware of the increased problems of social exclusion and the inequities which they observe both in their visualisation of some of the OECD scenarios and in the current situation. One area where inequities are observed is in the distribution of resources between Ontario's minority and majority education systems. Some participants are concerned that the scenarios resulting in privatisation could reduce access to education for students from less wealthy families; others are also concerned that performance standards or evaluation criteria that are too high or too inflexible could result in even greater exclusion of students with learning disabilities.

- Tend to incorporate, in their seventh scenario for the French-language School of the Future, issues related to immigration and diversity, the environment, and information and communication technologies.

- Were able, in their homogeneous groups, to ask in-depth questions about the roles of parents, students, teachers and principals in the context of the situations described in the scenarios and of a seventh scenario for the French-language school in 2020.

- Noted the changing nature of family and community life in their exploration of the OECD scenarios and took this into consideration in the development of the seventh scenario for the French-language School of the Future, and reflected on the impact of such changes on the link between the school, the family, and the community.

- Believed that the development of the seventh scenario for the French-language School of the Future generally enabled them to articulate the desired scenario and to identify the key elements of a shared vision of the French-language education of the future.

- Appreciated the opportunity to reflect on the future of the French-language school outside the usual context and its contradictions and to explore a variety of potential changes and directions in the development of French-language education.

Overall, the approach developed by *Vision 2020* enabled the participants to initiate dialogue, develop the capacity to reflect on possible or probable futures through the OECD scenarios and imagine the French-language School of the Future based on the shared values that were collectively considered essential and desirable.

## Unexpected outcomes of phase III of the Vision 2020 project

The consultations carried out so far have resulted in valuable outcomes which were not anticipated initially.

## Awareness of identity

The discussion by francophone students, teachers and parents of the future of French-language education and the challenges posed by the collective future is an opportunity for participants from various regions and ethno-cultural communities in the province to get to know one another better, to share their unique characteristics, their differences and their similarities, to discover what they have in common, and to become aware of what unites them. The process of exploring the OECD scenarios and developing a seventh scenario for the French-language School of the Future is in fact similar to collective action research which incorporates reflection on the features of a collective identity.

## Unanticipated transforming effects

Many participants say their participation in the *Vision 2020* forum prompted them to want to become more involved in the French-language education system. Others created exchange networks after the consultations to continue the reflection or take action as a group. These are indicators that the consultations could have a transforming effect on participants.

Furthermore, many participants spontaneously made a connection between the concept of the learning community in one of the OECD scenarios and the learning community that is part of the *Aménagement linguistique* policy. They also made the connection between the concept of schools as core social centres that appears in the OECD scenarios and strengthening the links between family, school and community advocated by the *Aménagement linguistique* policy by proposing structural changes in the seventh scenario conducive to establishing such connections.

## Initiatives prompted by participants

After the consultation with teachers, some participants decided to design and organise *Vision 2020* consultations in their elementary and secondary school classrooms. These initiatives are paving the way for the development of *Vision 2020* classroom learning tools. The Ministry and FESFO plan to reflect these experiences in the preparation of the *Vision 2020* Facilitation and Consultation Kit.

## Development of methods for planning and organising consultations

### The development of research tools

Once the facilitation approach had been determined, we developed the following tools to document and analyse the content of the consultations and highlight the vision of French-language education that emerged:

- A *Gabarit pour la cueillette de données*,[3] or data-collection template, for use by note-takers during consultations.

- A standard method for analysing consultations using analytical reports produced by the Ministry.

- A method for evaluating the facilitation process using a report written by FESFO after each consultation.

- A *Grille de comparaison des consultations Vision 2020*[4] used to map changes in the facilitation process and identify the analytical categories of the content of the consultations.

### The facilitation and consultation kit for education partners and community agencies

In the third phase of *Vision 2020*, we tested a new consultation and facilitation approach in the five consultations carried out across 2004 and 2005, and refined the process with the help of the evaluations from each consultation. Now we feel we can produce a definitive version of the process, in the form of a *Vision 2020* Facilitation and Consultation Kit which we would like to publish and distribute in 2006. The kit is intended to support our education partners and agencies in the francophone community in their reflection on the future of French-language education in Ontario.

---

[3] *Gabarit pour la cueillette de données lors des consultations Vision 2020 en 2005* (Template for Data Collection during *Vision 2020* Consultations in 2005), Working Document No. 2 (prepared by Monique Gauvin, consulting sociologist), Ontario Ministry of Education, French-Language Education Policy and Programs Branch, April 2005.

[4] *Tableaux synoptiques comparatifs des consultations/Grille de l'évolution du processus d'animation et des catégories d'analyse* (Comparative Synoptic Charts of Consultations/Grid Mapping Changes in the Facilitation Process and Analytical Categories), Draft No. 2 (prepared by Monique Gauvin, consulting sociologist), Ontario Ministry of Education, French-Language Education Policy and Programs Branch, February 14, 2005.

The kit must be flexible and geared to a democratic and inclusive approach. It could also include a *Vision 2020* learning tool for the classroom.

## Use of the OECD scenarios

During Phase III of *Vision 2020*, we gave the participants abridged versions of the OECD scenarios for use in the discussions. Since not all of the scheduled consultations have been completed, the following summary of participants' perceptions of the scenarios is incomplete and could change with upcoming consultations:

- For the time being, the preferred scenarios are still the "Schools as Core Social Centres" scenario and the "Schools as Focused Learning Organisations" scenario, which are generally considered more reflective of the values of the French-language schools.

- Thus far, the "Extending the Market Model" scenario does not appear to be part of a desirable future for the participants.

- Thus far, two scenarios are considered more relevant to the present than the future: the "Teacher Exodus" scenario and the "Bureaucratic School Systems Continue" scenario.

- Two scenarios are often discussed as solutions (the solution to something unacceptable in its current version): the "Teacher Exodus" scenario and the "Learning Networks and the Network Society" scenario.

The use of the OECD scenarios as a forward-thinking method and their exploration through the values filter encourage the participants to imagine themselves in probable or possible futures while reflecting on the values that the OECD scenarios convey and the potential impact of each scenario on the French-language school.

### *The seventh scenario for the French-language schools*

In their reflection on the seventh scenario for the French-language School of the Future, the participants have been able thus far to explore and identify what they consider the preferable or desirable future of the French-language school. The facilitation challenge has been to ensure the participants have enough time during the consultations to develop such a scenario and are provided with indicators in order to describe the scenario as clearly as possible. As the series of consultations continued, the categories of discussion that were used to help the participants describe the seventh scenario changed and eventually became the following questions:

- How would you describe the French-language School of the Future in terms of learning and its organisation, administration and governance, resources and infrastructure and teachers?
- What values are inherent in the seventh scenario for the French-language School of the Future?

For the time being, the summary description of the content of the seventh scenario, as created by the participants, appears in the analytical report produced for each consultation. We plan to use the comparative cumulative analysis of the consultation discourse to describe the vision of French-language education that emerges from the consultations as a group.

## *Vision 2020 and public policy development*

*Vision 2020* has changed and progressed to become, by the third phase, an extensive consultation project. In *Vision 2020*, the Ministry acts more as facilitator, partner and participant than absolute owner of the process. The Ministry also agreed to embark on a process in which not everything is pre-determined, and testing and research play a substantial part. But what link can be made between *Vision 2020* and public policy development?

In our opinion, the strongest link consists of taking a component that is often taken for granted in the public policy development process, and consulting and introducing an element of risk – the risk of placing oneself in a listening position and giving the floor to those who do not often have it in a school system that we claim must meet their needs. The results have often been strikingly authentic, fostered by an awareness of others' experience and the capacity within each person to effect change.

## *Vision 2020 and the "*Aménagement linguistique*" policy*

*Vision 2020* has taken place when the *Aménagement linguistique* policy was being implemented in the French-language district school boards. The policy promotes the building of a francophone identity and the development of participatory leadership through the establishment of learning communities, and advocates linguistic and cultural reproduction and the sustainable development of the French-language community through increased family/school/community partnerships or alliances.

While they are the product of an international initiative, the *Vision 2020* consultation forums are an arena for discussion on what a learning community in operation could be. They are also a place where ideas emerge concerning methods to implement for the structuring of such learning communities but also to strengthen the links between family, school and community in a context of globalisation, the development of information and communication technologies, and the development of a knowledge-based economy.

## Conclusion

In its vision statement, the Ontario Ministry of Education expresses the belief that in order to marshal widespread commitment and resourcefulness to deal with the most substantive education issues, it will strive to establish more interactive relations with its education partners and the public. Included in the four strategies the Ministry proposes for achieving such a vision is a reference to involving students, families and communities in the establishment of a positive learning environment.

*Vision 2020* has changed and progressed to become a consultation project in which participants are asked to take ownership of reflection on the future of schooling, and the consultation and facilitation approach is designed to encourage this ownership process and to create spaces and tools so that this ownership can take place. Consequently, *Vision 2020*, through its consultative and inclusive nature, is contributing to the development of a culture of partnership among the Ministry, the education partners and the community and, in this case, to the community's involvement in the definition of the future of its education system.

# Chapter 12
# Reflections on the practice and potential of futures thinking

by
Tom Bentley, Raymond Daigle, Walo Hutmachter, Hanne Shapiro
and Charles Ungerleider[1]

*The rapporteurs of the 2004 Toronto Forum (two Canadians, three Europeans) were called upon both to advance general priorities for futures thinking in education and were assigned to workshops on each of the volunteer systems described in Chapters 7-11. Their contributions show how convinced they are by the value of the futures thinking approach but they are also struck by the complexity as well as the difficulty of educational change. Ungerleider focuses on value questions. Daigle asks whether much current reform is often "tinkering at the edges", so that scenarios might help in more fundamental re-definitions. Hutmacher argues the need to consolidate the evidence base for such approaches and Shapiro calls for the scope of futures thinking stakeholders and methodologies to be broadened. Bentley distinguishes between and discusses the "inward-facing" and "outward-facing" aspects to futures thinking in action.*

The rapporteurs of the June 2004 Toronto Forum on "Schooling for Tomorrow" were sources of reflections and wisdom throughout the event, and they were assigned to workshops on each of the volunteer systems covered in the above chapters. Their reflections were based partly on the workshop discussions but they used their opportunities for reaction to raise more general issues about futures thinking in education. These reflections have been elaborated into the texts of this chapter.

---

[1] The rapporteurs to the Toronto "Schooling for Tomorrow" Forum.

Their contributions show how impressed they are in general by the different country initiatives; but they are also struck by the complexity as well as the difficulty of educational change, especially when the reforms in question are fundamental. The structures and practices of educational systems are supported by underlying, often strongly-held values. Much current reform is often "tinkering at the edges" instead of re-defining schooling, while some of the most important changes are unintentional and forced upon the system by external developments. One theme coming through this chapter is that using scenarios offers a possibility for a more intentional and fundamental discussion on reforming the system, opening up new avenues not just rehearsing pre-existing options. One prerequisite for this is robust analytical tools. A related theme identified is the need to understand better and more systematically the trends that are driving change in educational systems. A desirable way forward is also that the futures thinking should engage a wide range of stakeholders in education in the dialogue on reform. These authors can see, if these and related conditions are met, that scenarios can be invaluable tools for strategic insight and help provide the catalyst for genuine reform.

## Futures thinking to clarify value differences (Charles Ungerleider[2])

Futures thinking facilitates dialogue and fosters the consideration of policy alternatives. It does so by helping the different stakeholders engaged in it to transcend the positional politics that typically and necessarily accompany the consideration of policy alternatives intended for immediate implementation. Freed from the encapsulation that immediacy imposes, it allows participants to explore possibilities collectively, consider the consequences of various possibilities, and test the boundaries of policy options under various conditions.

One form of futures thinking involves the use of scenarios that depict conditions twenty or thirty years in the future. Such scenarios have been used in the OECD "Schooling for Tomorrow" project conducted under the auspices of the OECD as a set of "tools" to help policy makers and practitioners respond to significant changes affecting education. The intention is to develop capacity for the management of change in education and other public policy domains on an international basis. Part of my assignment as rapporteur at the Toronto Forum was to observe the New

---

[2] Professor of Sociology of Education, University of British Columbia (UBC), Vancouver, Canada.

Zealand "Secondary Futures" project and three dimensions they presented were particularly interesting.

The first involved the use of "Guardians", a group of four nationally recognised persons responsible for "protecting the integrity of the process" and ensuring its autonomy from government as well as from short term policy and labour relations disputes. Second, New Zealand rewrote the original scenarios developed by the OECD in language designed to make them easily understood by the various audiences of New Zealanders who would be involved in workshops. In addition, New Zealand developed "character narratives" to enable participants to view the scenario from the perspective of various positions: student, parent, teacher, etc. This particularly useful technique allows those who use the scenarios to "walk in the shoes" of fictional New Zealanders. The "character narratives" help participants to recognise that scenarios are likely to be viewed differently by persons occupying different social positions. A third element being developed by New Zealand to support its work is a "preference matrix", a device to enable participants to specify the desirable features of schooling options.

It is as true in education as in any domain that no matter how much a change is needed or wanted, if those who do the work do not want the change, it will be unlikely to occur without significant social or economic costs. Teachers, and the organisations that represent teachers, are often neglected in the consideration of policy changes in education, viewed as marginal to the change process, or seen in a negative light as obstacles to be overcome. It was refreshing to see included in the New Zealand delegation representatives of their teachers. Attention to the perspectives that teachers bring to their responsibilities is particularly important, since educational change has often neglected to see and appreciate the process from their perspectives.

An implicit and largely unexamined assumption of futures thinking is the notion that educational change is an inherent good but it is desirable only if that change is intentional. Too often, the changes that occur are a consequence of circumstance rather than conscious deliberation. It is equally important to recognise that education is an essentially conservative influence that provides a stabilising force in societies characterised by periods of rapid change in other spheres of human activity. Education helps us to locate ourselves in time and place and to understand how we are related to others. New Zealand includes indigenous peoples among the "Guardians". The Guardians ensure the integrity of the futures thinking process by recognising the potential that futures thinking has for destabilising societies contemplating changes to accommodate future conditions.

While still embryonic, futures thinking holds promise as a means for exploring policy options. As techniques are developed for bringing policy analysts and decision makers together to consider the future, it will be important to safeguard against a technical view of policy. By this I mean that some may believe that futures thinking will reveal "good" public policy. To state the obvious: What counts as "good" policy is a matter of the values one holds, not a quality of the policy itself. Nothing of value in public affairs is apolitical. In fact, it is the clash of values that gives rise to the need for politics and policy. Future scenario planning is useful for exploring the nature of value conflicts. But the technique will not yield policies that can be implemented without regard to the context in which the policies may be needed or to the values at play in those contexts.

Values are often incommensurable, making it impossible to realise the full expression of all the values held. Take five illustrative values – universality, productive efficiency, equity, accountability, and flexibility – commonly associated rhetorically with education systems in many jurisdictions:

- *Universality* is concerned with ensuring that all children of school age are able to attend and benefit from public schooling.

- *Productive efficiency* is concerned with producing the maximum benefits possible for the given expenditure of public monies.

- *Equity* is concerned that expenditures are made to reduce gaps between identifiable groups of students (boys and girls, native-born and immigrant, Aboriginal and non-Aboriginal, rich and poor, etc.).

- *Accountability* is concerned with reporting to the public about how resources it provided have been used to achieve the goals of public schooling.

- *Flexibility* is concerned with permitting the widest possible latitude in decisions about the expenditure of funds. Although people might prize all of these values, all five cannot be fully realised simultaneously.

We have long recognised that "change" and "structure" are in tension. Structures and practices are supported by underlying values. Proposals for change carry the implicit repudiation of the values that support the practice or structure one is proposing to change. A proposal to alter a practice or structure is also a proposal to replace the existing value or values with new ones.

One of the dimensions not fully explored in futures thinking is a specification of the values that support existing practices and structures.

Different values are discernible in the various scenarios. New Zealand's attempt to develop a "preference matrix" is a useful and promising step. Other jurisdictions and their initiatives should consider this example by devoting explicit attention to *identifying* the value differences and *comparing the ranks* attached to them in various scenarios. This process should lead to interesting insights about differences in the scenarios and a deeper understanding of the important part that values play in determining practices and structures.

I have already noted that the futures thinking process is often employed to free participants from the spatial and temporal constraints that inhibit the consideration of alternatives. This is both a benefit and a liability of the process. Freedom from such constraints is likely to help generate innovative alternatives. That same freedom can also mislead participants into believing that one can arrive at a goal or destination without an appreciation of one's starting point. Change requires an appreciation of the temporal and spatial location in which one is situated and the factors that gave rise to the structures and practices one wants to alter. Dissatisfaction with a state of affairs is insufficient for bringing about change. In order to change the prevailing state of affairs, one needs an analysis of how it came to be and the values that support its continuation.

Futures thinking can help to develop the capacity for technical analysis and the understanding of systems. This is "systems thinking", which can help to inform policy development, but cannot and should not supplant the political processes of the jurisdictions that employ the technique. The factors affecting politicians are different from those that affect policy analysts. Failure to recognise and appreciate the differences can lead to unhelpful tension and distrust between policy analysts and politicians. Such a tendency might be mitigated by making explicit the discussion and ranking of values. It might also be mitigated by accompanying futures thinking with simulation exercises that put policy analysts and politicians into situations that demand their interaction.

## Do schools need to be reformed or reinvented? (Raymond Daigle[3])

For the past 15 years or so, a number of industrialised countries have been implementing sweeping and costly reforms aimed at ensuring that future generations are adequately prepared for the new knowledge-based economy. In all the OECD countries, the expression "lifelong learning" and

---

[3] Former Deputy Minister, Francophone Sector, New Brunswick, Canada and Member of the Advisory Board to the Ontario *Vision 2020* initiative.

its many variants have been used to excess in all the official documents of the various bodies responsible for education at all levels. However, despite all these efforts, it must be admitted that these reforms have by and large met with only limited success. Although there was some real initial progress, these reforms have ultimately come up against a wall, or rather a ceiling, beyond which further progress seems impossible, leading increasing numbers of school administrators and educators to wonder whether schools do not need to be reformed but to be reinvented.

The fact is that reforming any public institution is a difficult task, and even more so if the institution is to be completely redefined. The task will be virtually insurmountable if the reform exercise is conducted by persons who are closely involved in the institution – which we all are as educational policy people and experts – for there are no other models available besides the one that we know. This exercise of reinventing schools and creating the necessary tools is therefore a daunting and complex task. It is for this reason that the OECD has designed scenarios in order to assist those responsible for education systems in carrying out this task. It must be pointed out that scenarios are not familiar tools for educators, as they are not widely used outside military organisations and certain business sectors. However, given the inability of school reforms to make further progress, there was justification for trying this exercise and seeing where it might lead. For example, one of the lead countries in the OECD project, the Netherlands, has in recent years adopted an innovative national policy for primary and secondary education that is currently being implemented on three fronts:

- Central government's relationship with educational institutions: deregulation and greater freedom for institutions within more general central government policies.

- Quality of education (learner-centred education, educational research, the social role of schools, their environment and setting) as a means of strengthening the economy and citizenship.

- Professional development for teachers and school management in order to develop the educational leadership role of school heads and make the teaching profession more attractive.

Under this policy, networks formed in each sector are developing a four-year action plan starting from a commonly defined vision. In the course of this initiative, it appears that the scenario approach was abandoned, those involved having found the scenarios too futuristic (too speculative and extremely long term) and at times contradictory, but chiefly because they found that these scenarios would not allow them to take action soon enough. This reaction is understandable given that the entire exercise is primarily focused on meeting the objectives set by the European Community for 2010, which are aimed at making Europe the most competitive knowledge-based economy in the world and ensuring its social cohesion. In this context, thinking about the future becomes much more immediate. A number of the countries present in the workshop I was rapporteur for also admitted that all their energies were currently focused on the European Community's objectives. What is more, not all countries have reached the same stage in this process. Each country's background, history, traditions and values significantly affect the approaches and procedures used and have a major impact on educational reforms. For example, some countries, such as Finland, already have long-term forward-looking mechanisms integrated into their parliamentary and governmental institutions that make the exercise considerably easier to conduct.

Although the approaches and strategies under way in the Netherlands are valid, interesting, and solidly co-ordinated, they focus on the same major aspects of reform (pupil-centred education, educational research, indicators, measurement, leadership by school heads, teacher training, etc.) that several other countries have been targeting in recent years (*e.g.* the United Kingdom, the United States, Canada, etc.), and may therefore come up against the same obstacles. Consequently, this exercise has yet to lead to genuine long-term "futures thinking" and, above all, it has not resulted in a real re-definition or reinvention of schools. "We are tinkering at the edges", futurologists might say.

Furthermore, listening to all the participants in the Toronto Forum gave the impression that most participating countries are encountering difficulties in actually using the scenarios, with some countries rejecting them outright as a tool, while others are content to work on the scenario or scenarios of their own preference, sometimes dismissing out of hand the other scenarios even though in some cases these are much more likely to occur – perhaps choosing to see the future through rose-tinted glasses? Maybe we should allow specialists more accustomed to working with scenarios than educators to share their expertise and experience with them. Otherwise, there is a risk that at the end of the exercise we will reject the scenario method as marginal or at best inconclusive, thereby depriving ourselves of a tool that might prove to be extremely useful.

In the meantime, serious, large-scale efforts are under way, but which run the risk of having only a temporary and limited impact on the capacity of education systems to prepare the next generation to work in the new knowledge-based economy. Cynics could ask whether those responsible for educational reform have found it in their interest to limit the scope of school reforms since they would have much to lose if the current systems were to disappear.

## Consolidate the foundations of evidence-based futures thinking (Walo Hutmacher[4])

The lead countries in the recent phase of the OECD "Schooling for Tomorrow" project have been very active and developed interesting projects and contributions. They also have quite legitimately introduced their own agendas into the programme. It is no surprise therefore that the different projects do not easily combine into a systematic pattern. This kind of futures thinking is also rather new in the education sector and there is little agreed methodology. The understanding of futures thinking may differ considerably across constituencies and among individual participants.

A common feature across the projects is nevertheless that, from the material published earlier in "What Schools for the Future?" (OECD, 2001), they have promptly adopted the scenarios and/or the scenario method. The published scenarios indeed cover a range of alternative futures: despite the fact that only two of them have consistently been considered desirable in educational circles, they were found useful to widen the intellectual horizon and the scope of futures thinking. Some constituencies have elaborated new scenarios of their own. The scenario method has been mainly used to date in this context to sketch change or innovation agendas, be it to increase leadership skills of managers and school leaders as in England, or to discuss about "what secondary schooling should be like in the future" as in New Zealand, or to meet the "threat of assimilation" on the French minority language community as in Ontario. The wide range of the themes, by the way, underlines the diversity of specific needs and interests in futures thinking in the education field.

There has been less work on and little reference to the analytical dimensions of the scenarios. With the exception of the Ontario project on teachers and teaching, there has also been little emphasis on clarifying or deepening our understanding of the major trends and forces that underpin the change of education systems, of schools and of education policies in relation with the change of society, culture and economy. Overall, the culture and practice in education systems seem to make it difficult to take the time needed for a non-normative and systematic description and analysis of different possible futures, and the considered argumentation of their likelihood in the light of societal change. The projects in the second phase seem more interested in the desirable, rather than in possible and likely,

---

[4] Professor Emeritus, Faculty of Psychology and Educational Sciences, University of Geneva, Switzerland.

futures. What should or should not happen is more appealing than what might happen.

Any debate in the education field, of course, ultimately challenges values, which are often conflicting. Historically, this has been the main thrust of the debate about the future of education and schools: opinions and wishes opposing other opinions and wishes. The debate about values will also remain in the future. But the new brand of futures thinking which the OECD programme aims at developing differs from that tradition mainly by adopting a two-stage approach. The first question here is not "what future do we wish?" but "towards what future does or might the education field move, considering recent and/or likely economic, technological, cultural and societal developments?" In other words, while the desirability debate certainly must take place, it should do so at a second stage only and on the basis of a prior systematic effort to explore possible futures and their likelihood. It should do this on premises that remain as descriptive and analytical as possible.

The basic assumption is indeed that education systems and schools are actually changing and will change in the future, that they are actually heading somewhere, because their environment changes. A better knowledge of societal, demographic, cultural and/or economic trends and forces, which are in relationship with education in families, communities and schools, should help identify with better accuracy this "unplanned" or "spontaneous" but nevertheless real change. It will help to understand its likely impact on schools and their possible and likely ways of coping with what confronts them.

For the future of futures thinking, including within the OECD "Schooling for Tomorrow" project, it seems important therefore to identify and discuss more precisely the configuration of social, cultural and economic trends and forces that contribute to change of the education field through constituencies, institutions and organisations. The original analysis of trends and driving forces in Part One and several expert contributions in Part Two of "What Schools for the Future" (OECD, 2001) gave a first flavour of such a knowledge base and they have loosely informed the dimensions that structure the scenarios. But overall, this conceptual and analytical basis has not been at the forefront during the previous phase. This CERI programme has the mission to elaborate a framework for futures thinking in the education field that will be useful across countries. The quality of this framework will depend on how much effort goes into clarifying, deepening and refining the conceptual grounds we build on. The programme should concentrate part of its efforts on developing a more robust (minimal, sufficient and arguable) conceptual framework and the related empirical knowledge base that will be able to shed light onto the complex relationships which exist between economy, society and education in families and schools.

## Broadening horizons, approaches and participants in futures thinking (Hanne Shapiro[5])

*"He who never leaves his country is full of prejudices"*
Carlo Goldoni (1703-1793), Pamela I, 14.

In the 1950s the United States invested heavily in order to be the leading country in transatlantic transportation. The *SS United States* was regarded as an imminent success and positive sign that the development was heading in the right direction; the speed of sea transportation was increased by a couple of miles per hour. Shortly after, the first commercial jet went in the air, and the previous so-important record for which enormous resources had been invested was suddenly reduced to only a minor role. The story can be likened to a situation where we only rely on measuring and benchmarking properties of knowledge acquisition – codifiable and viewed as important of today – and risk ignoring other components of knowledge acquisition and learning that may be vital to our societies of tomorrow.

Can we afford unilateral thinking about our schooling system which in most cases at best will lead to incremental improvements? Currently there is much policy debate about the emergence of a so-called knowledge economy or learning economy, still relatively undefined terms. Do we therefore need a much more radical, proactive, and experimenting approach to the development and governance of our learning systems with a broader involvement of actors than we traditionally see within educational policy formulation processes?

Education and the broader notion of schooling as a social system have developed over a long period of time in each country with specific sets of institutions and organisations. (Institutions can be defined as sets of common habits, routines, rules, or laws, which regulate the relations and interactions between individuals and groups. Organisations are formal structures with an explicit purpose; they are consciously created and can thus also be changed as a result of social action [Edquist and Johnson, 1997].) Governments, educational organisations, communities, business and industry, and unions, have constructed an institutional set-up for education and schooling which in many instances has undergone so little change so as

---

[5] Head of Centre, Policy Analysis and Innovation, Danish Technological Institute, Aarhus, Denmark.

to become ossified, deeply rooted in already existing social, cultural, and economic patterns. Because of these roots, educational institutions and practices are difficult to change, and are sometimes even obstacles to innovation of the broader system of schooling and learning.

The embedded systemic resistance to change and the uncertainties relating to changes in the outer environment and the impacts those may have on the future of schooling mean that policy-making for the future of schooling cannot be treated as a straightforward linear process. This is also why policy-making should adopt other more qualitative methods for engaging with alternative realities of the futures in a manner that can bring us out of perceived realities and urgencies of action.

The *raison d'être* for engaging in the future of the schooling voyage is not to get strategic and operational guidance on how to travel from A to B – your preferred neighbourhood destination – in the shortest period of time. Rather, through futures thinking, participants embark on a voyage of exploration into unknown areas and beyond. Like Alice in Wonderland when she falls down the rabbit hole, you soon realise that conventional wisdom and solutions are not going to be much help on this journey. Scenario analysis should be regarded as a tool for insight and a catalyst for strategic discussions and reflections on policy dilemmas, but not as an end in itself for policy implementation. The connection between the use of futures thinking for questioning and for exploring challenging policy questions, and methods relating to creative strategic policy implementation, needs to be explored further The experience from the Toronto Forum suggests that the problems-formulation phase – the questions that are to be addressed through the scenario work – should receive more attention.

A futures initiative should not be merely a comfortable ride in a relatively known local neighbourhood, but should bring participants to areas they never imagined might exist. Prerequisites for this are a consistent and wide-ranging environmental scanning, of both the outer world and the nearby environment, not merely the latter. It also asks for a structured analysis of trends, drivers, and uncertainties and forces relating to these trends. A methodology such as TAIDA is an example of how approaches to trend spotting and trend analysis can be expanded as part of the range of methods in its future developments. The methodology is based on the EPISTEL+ M framework for identifying trends and to scan in a systematic and comprehensive way. (EPISTEL+M is a way of clustering trends: E=economy; P=politics; S=social values; T=technology; E= environment, health; L=legislation + M=media and ideology.) Trends need to be apparent for a certain amount of time; otherwise they are fluctuations and may have little impact in the long run. Trends have a direction: *more, less, the same*, and they have a degree of certainty and uncertainty. Given the tendency for futures initiatives to move too quickly to a preferred scenario, the OECD "Schooling for Tomorrow" project could usefully identify different methods of analysis, such as cross-impact analysis, mapping trends according to the level of importance and level of certainty with regard to the question addressed in the given scenario exercise.

Changing schooling and education is not only a matter of changing the educational system, but also of innovating wider socio-economic system, cultural mindsets, and governance frameworks. This is an important observation for understanding the design and revitalisation of schooling systems. Policies for change cannot be organised top-down. Change in schooling has to be directed simultaneously at all the levels. Interactivity and consistency between the different layers are main requirements for systemic change. The government and its administration is but one of the players in a complex policy system such as schooling; so are schools, teachers, parents, unions, and other policy domains, all fighting for attention in the battle of scarce resources.

This suggests that futures thinking should not only involve educationalists within the social system of schooling, but also other actors from the broader socio-economic environment with different mindsets and backgrounds, so as to avoid being captured by conventional wisdoms about what lies ahead and to ensure a wider horizon and unconventional questions throughout the whole process.

Systems change is not a one-shot event. Change in most social systems is an on-going process of incremental development, sometimes combined with earthquakes (dissipative systems: absorbing a lot of change-impulses without any change; then disrupting in a large change; see Sanderson, 2000). Changing a system is a time-consuming endeavour, especially because of institutional embeddedness. Reasons for change can be endogenous and exogenous. Systems change is complex and chaotic because of it is multi-layered, multi-actor, and multi-purpose.

Process competencies are therefore central to facilitate a futures activity. Futures thinking initiatives within countries require a guidance and process training package as a component of the "toolbox" of approaches. In a well-facilitated process, as developed by England and demonstrated during the Toronto Forum, different actors can come into play through a futures process despite different backgrounds and mindsets. Through this process they may explore the outer galaxies (environmental scanning) and discover how they are actually part of the sun-earth interaction (the schooling system). Managing this process is like directing a large orchestra; if one player is out of tune, the whole performance is endangered.

The use of metaphors is another essential component of a successful process in order to avoid being trapped in current realities and concepts. A simple methodology to encourage participants to break with their traditional roles is the use of "hot seating" – where participants are required to take up another character role. This method is simple, efficient, and fun, as the England workshop illustrated. The concepts of *performance text* (Collins, 1990) derived from ethnographical studies and theatre may be useful in framing futures thinking processes. Through the act of co-participation these works bring the audience into and revitalise the space of action.

## *Futures thinking for policy change*

Studies on the nature of policy change have traditionally taken their point of departure in the so-called policy cycle where the policy process is analysed as set in different distinct stages: decision-making, implementation, and evaluation. The learning approach to policy formulation as brought forward by researchers such as Lundvall criticises this assumption because it does not provide a thorough account of what happens after the decision-making phase and it tends to perceive change as something automatic that follows the political decision-making process (Lundvall, 1997). The learning approach on the other hand provides a more fluid perspective on the policy process in continuous transformation and evolution where no clear stages can be discerned.

> *"In the political environment of public management, learning processes are particular difficult to create and maintain. A critical task of public management is to build institutional learning capabilities within the system of actors. Conventional policy processes often block learning because ideology overrides evidence or vested interests resist. Therefore policy makers should be concerned with designing adaptable innovation systems - rather than producing blueprints for specific reforms."* (Metcalfe, 1993, quoted by Lundvall, 2000)

One of the advantages of using futures thinking for policy purposes is that it can create an arena where the same plot (schooling in the future) may be enacted through quite different scripts and with a stage populated by different characters and acting methods. Through narratives and dialogues that speak to both head and heart, the Toronto workshop has illustrated how the different methodologies may function as props which can further critical and creative reflection and revisualisation of a policy question ahead of us, rather than falling back on a traditional, one-dimensional and linear decisions-making process. This understanding of futures thinking as a multi-actor learning and visualisation process is central to the next stages of project's development, where broader issues concerning governance and underlying values around the knowledge economy and learning society should be addressed.

The OECD "Schooling for Tomorrow" project has proved itself successful to date in involving school leaders, teachers, and parents, in envisioning change. The next stage of the project will need to address more deeply how the futures methodologies and approaches can also engage policy makers in critically and creatively exploring medium-term policy choices and dilemmas, given that policy constituencies most often will judge the success of policy makers on short-term successes which may fix a particular bolt but not lead to safer, faster, or cheaper forms of transportation. This is the challenge for the OECD "Schooling of Tomorrow" project.

## Using futures thinking strategically: inward and outward-facing processes (Tom Bentley[6])

The Toronto Forum on "Schooling for Tomorrow" showed how different the emphasis of different futures projects can be, not just in context and content, but also through the variation of participants and intended audiences. One of the basic differences to emerge was that between futures processes which face primarily *inwards,* and those which face *outwards,* towards the public and practitioners. All OECD "Schooling for Tomorrow" projects of course seek a broad, long term view of the issues they are addressing, but their focus and methods do vary in this way.

*Inward–facing* futures work seeks to think differently from a policy perspective about long-term issues which go beyond the scope of existing reform plans and implementation timetables. Their potential lies in uncovering and strengthening a more strategic view of the goals and methods of reform; helping policy makers understand the range of factors – from technological innovation to changing demographics – which will influence the success of their measures and provide new means with which to achieve their goals.

Those which face *outwards* are seeking to engage a wider set of stakeholders and participants in a dialogue which might help to uncover solutions or innovations that were previously treated as being out of bounds for political or historical reasons. They may well seek the same kind of long view and strategic analysis as inward facing processes, but their goals are

---

[6] Director, Demos, the London-based think-tank.

also about stimulating new forms of dialogue, creating legitimacy for change, and involving new participants in the process.

Any long-term effort at reshaping or reforming education systems depends on both inward- and outward-looking processes, and a number of OECD "Schooling for Tomorrow" projects are arguably tackling both. But the experience so far suggests that it is worth clarifying the differences and reflecting on how different elements of the process can be combined successfully.

Education and schooling systems are increasingly understood as being complex systems – efforts at reform must cope with the complexity of implementation, and schools must serve a more complex and diverse society. Developing the capacity to adapt continuously, and to differentiate according to variation in context and in student need, is a priority for reformers across the OECD, fuelling the search for innovation techniques and strategies. But many innovative solutions are potentially blocked, not by a lack of technical means to make them happen, but by a lack of legitimacy or political support among key stakeholders in the education system, such as parents, trade unions, employers, higher education and so on. In turn, schooling systems which rest on highly institutionalised structures and routines also create expectations and roles – for all of these groups and more – which are deeply entrenched and difficult to adapt. In other words, policy can get stuck, and the role of different players in the system can also get stuck; unsticking both is a necessary condition of systemic change.

Reshaping complex systems maintained by many different stakeholders requires that all such stakeholders need to participate in a shift of perspective which uncovers new solutions and affirms the value of collective adaptation. One argument is that, in order for this to happen, all those key participants must be involved in creating a new shared view of the system, its goals, and how it can work. Traditionally, this kind of task is tackled through formal consultation processes. But, in many systems, such consultation is either marginal to the process of policy formation, or treated as an extension of interest group politics – that is, different organisations and groups participate in it but with closed minds, articulating fixed positions which represent their current place in the current system, but refusing to engage with new possibilities which would require a different set of roles and relationships in order to succeed.

Using futures thinking to unlock new policy options requires a methodical process which sets long-term trends and possible changes in the operating environment against the existing policy commitments and longer-term goals of a specific system. It needs to be informed by trend data, by comparative analysis, and by examples of innovation which help to extend the boundaries of imagination. The use of scenarios in this kind of exercise can be a trigger for thinking differently about existing policy, and can feed into planning and strategy processes in ways which enrich them.

To succeed, policy makers need two conditions to occur simultaneously. First, they need the trend and scenario analysis to be robust and relevant to their detailed operational concerns – something which requires careful, focused work and is not guaranteed by the existence of broad, impressionistic scenarios, however well grounded they are. Second, policy makers need to engage with the issues in a setting which enables them to be candid and open-minded about their existing commitments, something which is extremely difficult for both public servants and politicians in today's pressured times. These conditions imply a degree of privacy and discretion around the discussions, even if they lead to published material and public debate later on.

Aspects of this inward looking emphasis can be found in a number of the OECD "Schooling for Tomorrow" initiatives, from Ontario to New Zealand, England to the Netherlands, where senior policy makers have been deeply engaged in futures workshops and in discussing the value of longer term thinking to education reform more widely. But some of the conditions needed for success stand in contrast to those of outward-facing futures processes. Outward facing processes seek to address the same big questions about the form and function of our schooling systems, but to do it in a way which engages a wider range of perspectives, and enables them to shape an approach to change which could generate a wider range of solutions.

From the discussions at the Toronto Forum, it became clear that addressing concerns and anxieties among groups external to government was a crucial dimension of establishing successful futures processes, in every participating system. Thus, for example in New Zealand, the impact of a previous generation of public sector reform had left education trade unions deeply suspicious of new reform efforts, and determined to protect their members against unexpected change or policies whose impact had not been fully thought through. In Canada, new thinking about how to provide education for the Francophone community had to involve key representatives of that community, as well as other institutional stakeholders, if it was going to establish the basic legitimacy needed for new designs to be treated as possible solutions.

Establishing genuine dialogue among the different participant groups is, in fact, a challenge in itself – dialogue in which all participants positions and affiliations command respect, but in which key assumptions about change can remain suspended, or open, in order for a wider range of possible solutions to emerge. In the Futuresight process, for example, used by the

English team to work with school leaders and other practitioners, participants were engaged and motivated by the materials but found working with an agenda in which the end point was not predetermined an unfamiliar experience. Many said that if final policy destinations had been presented to them they would respond to them in "pre-programmed" ways, on the basis of their past experience. Working in a more open-ended process and being confronted with the trade-offs and conflicts between different trends and elements of different scenarios helped to equip practitioners to translate some of the difficult choices back into their own school development processes, and to engage in debate with policy makers on new terms.

Even these projects, however, faced outwards primarily towards existing education practitioners. Arguably, futures thinking projects need to go further if they are to help establish new space and legitimacy for system change – into the expectations and responses of the wider public. For example, in the Demos project Scotland 2020 (report available at www.demos.co.uk) a "town meeting" was held in Nairn, a small highland town, in which local residents used open space methods to generate a set of priorities for the future which could be communicated to policy makers. In the successor project, Glasgow 2020, the aim is to undertake "an exercise in mass imagination" through a range of events, art and literature projects, and other media through which people communicate ideas, aspirations and perceptions of the city and its possible future.

This kind of public engagement is essential to the prospects of long term systemic change in education. But the detailed work that it requires is quite different from that involved in building a sharper, systemic view of possible futures among policy makers struggling with the pressures of today and tomorrow. This fact suggests that we also need further discussion of the nuances of project design for futures processes – and a clearer understanding of how different elements and layers of futures thinking work can be combined and integrated to address the different groups of participants identified by the OECD "Schooling for Tomorrow" participant projects.

One final practice, generated by New Zealand, provides a fitting conclusion. By appointing "Guardians" – independent, respected figures from New Zealand society – as an integral part of the Secondary Futures project, the team simultaneously created a point of engagement with New Zealanders in general, and created a safer space in which education stakeholders could enter into dialogue about possible futures. The existence of Guardians, a concept itself drawn from Aboriginal New Zealand tradition, reinforced the connection between an internal space and an external set of perspectives, and has enhanced the success of the project's engagement with a range of communities. It may be that our national education dialogues need better guardians, and that the next generation of OECD "Schooling for Tomorrow" projects can help to provide them.

# *References*

Collins P.H. (1990), *Black Feminist Thought. Knowledge Consciousness and the Politics of Empowerment*, Routledge, Chapman and Hall.

Edquist, C. and B. Johnson (1997), "Institutions and Organisations in Systems of Innovation", in C. Edquist (ed.), *Systems of Innovation: Technologies, Institutions and Organisations*, Cassel.

Lundvall, B.-Å. (1997), "Skærpet konkurrence, organisatorisk fornyelse og ændrede kvalifikationskrav", in A. Næss Gjerding (ed.), *Den fleksible virksomhed* (The Flexible Firm), Erhvervsudviklingsrådet, Copenhaguen.

Lundvall B.-Å. (2000), "Europe and the Learning Economy – On the Need for Reintegrating the Strategies of Firms, Social Partners and Policy-makers", Dept of Business Studies, Aalborg University, *www.druid.dk*

Metcalfe, L. (1993), "Public Management: From Imitation to Innovation", in J. Kooiman (ed.), *Modern Governance: New Government-society Interactions*, Sage, London.

OECD (2001), *What Schools for the Future?*, OECD, Paris.

Sanderson, I. (2000), "Evaluation in Complex Policy Systems", *Evaluation*, Vol. 6, No. 4, pp. 433-455.

# Also available in the CERI collection

*Personalising Education*
128 pages • February 2006 • ISBN: 92-64-03659-8

*Students with Disabilities, Learning Difficulties and Disadvantages – Statistics and Indicators*
152 pages • October 2005 • ISBN: 92-64-00980-9

*E-learning in Tertiary Education: Where do We Stand?*
290 pages • June 2005 • ISBN: 92-64-00920-5

*Formative Assessment – Improving Learning in Secondary Classrooms*
280 pages • February 2005 • ISBN: 92-64-00739-3

*Quality and Recognition in Higher Education: The Cross-border Challenge*
205 pages • October 2004 • ISBN: 92-64-01508-6

*Internationalisation and Trade in Higher Education* – *Opportunities and Challenges*
250 pages • June 2004 • ISBN: 92-64-01504-3

*Innovation in the Knowledge Economy* – *Implications for Education and Learning*
Knowledge Management series
96 pages • May 2004 • ISBN: 92-64-10560-3

www.oecdbookshop.org

OECD PUBLICATIONS, 2, rue André-Pascal, 75775 PARIS CEDEX 16
PRINTED IN FRANCE
(96 2006 05 1 P) ISBN 92-64-02363-1 – No. 55083 2006